How to Improve
the High School Band Sound

How to Improve
the
High School Band Sound

Russell A. Pizer

Parker Publishing Company
West Nyack, New York

Library of Congress Cataloging in Publication Data

Pizer, Russell A
   How to improve the high school band sound.

   1. Bands (Music)—Instruction and study.
I. Title.
MT733.P633   785'.06'707   75-28004
ISBN 0-13-413120-7

Printed in the United States of America

Dedicated to

George Cavender

. . . . for his contagious enthusiasm and abiding interest in those involved in bands and band music.

Also by the author:

ADMINISTERING THE ELEMENTARY BAND: Teaching Beginning Instrumentation and Developing a Band Support Program

How You Will Benefit from This Book

In this book you will find many step-by-step methods for improving the sound of the high school band in the following ten critical areas: balanced instrumentation, seating arrangements, sectional proportions and considerations, instrument usages, rehearsal procedures, warm-up routines, tuning procedures, as well as methods and procedures to follow for improving intonation, precision and musicianship.

In Chapter 1, you will find a clear definition of the differences between a so-called "military band," a symphonic band, a concert band and a wind ensemble. Based on this definition, specifics are given for choosing the type and number of instruments to use within the framework of the kinds, numbers and combinations of instruments on hand in any school so that compositions can be played with musical authenticity whether the band numbers 25 or 125. Because the sound of a band is determined to a great extent by the proportions of instruments within the individual sections, suggestions are given on how to maintain a desired instrumentation over a sustained period of years.

Chapter 2 gives the importance of seating arrangements, not only for the band as a whole but also for individual sections. The chapter tells you why it is necessary to evaluate the seating arrangements periodically. It shows methods for improving the effectiveness of the individual sections and different ways in which a better quality of sound might be produced through re-arranging the individuals within a section. It discusses the age-old problem of trumpet vs. cornet, baritone vs. euphonium and tuba vs. sousaphone, and how the choice results in the type of sound produced by the band.

Chapter 3 deals with the pre-planning of a rehearsal and provides guidelines for carrying on an effective rehearsal. It gives many suggestions on how to approach a rehearsal so that it is in fact a "rehearsal" and not just another play-through. It even suggests musical E.S.P. ideas that go a long way toward saving time and improving the overall sound of the band.

Chapter 4 discusses warm-up and tune-up procedures including the possible use of notes other than the standard B-flat concert. It gives several alternative tuning routines so that this part of the rehearsal can be a period for awakening the bandsmen's ears and not a day-dreaming period with air coming out of the end of the instrument. There are also suggested non-written warm-up routines that give the director a chance to sharpen up the band's following skills as well as his own baton technique.

Chapter 5 takes the reader through the band section by section and tells what must be done to obtain the best possible tone quality. This includes a discussion of what makes for good tone quality, not only in the woodwind and brass sections, but in the percussion section as well. It shows how to get a "good" sound out of such instruments as triangles and cymbals. Even the lowly triangle's tone must be considered. This chapter gives some constructive steps to be taken in this area. For example, an indication for the cymbals to be struck together *fortissimo* is not an indication for an unmusical, ear-shattering "crash," but for a tone that "fits into" the overall sound or enhances a climactic point. The discussion shows you how the percussion section blends into the overall tone quality of the band.

Chapter 6 tells how to approach the whole problem of intonation. It gives the reader some idea of the myriad of problems involved in creating better intonation within the band and the individual sections. The chapter includes some detailed figures on intonation problems in an effort to point out the complexity of the problem. It gives some insight into the problem of how dynamics affect intonation and how proper mechanical adjustments of instruments can help improve intonation, as well as some exercises on developing listening cues. Positive steps can be taken by the band director toward teaching the band the art of critical listening.

Chapter 7 discusses balance within the ensemble, precision and accuracy. This chapter tells the band director exactly how to develop and correct inaccuracy and imbalance both for himself and on the part of individual students. For example, this chapter contains a formula for acquiring better balance—a section that should be memorized by every member of the band. The section on tempo phenomenon will help any band improve the rhythmic drive of a march if followed accurately by the conductor.

Chapter 8 shows that good musicianship can be taught successfully. It is not that "certain something" that some "have" and some "haven't." The chapter provides specific steps to be taken to make the band play like a "professional" group, whether it be a simple 6/8 march or the *1812 Overture.*

Russell A. Pizer

Table of Contents

13

one

Establishing a Balanced Instrumentation

When the band director looks down from his podium at the time of the first rehearsal, he finds himself surrounded by a group of individuals with instruments in their hands. The methods, technics and attitudes he is able to bring to this and future rehearsals and inculcate into the minds and fingers of those before him determine whether they remain individuals or become welded into a group called a "band."

A band is not just a group of individuals; it is a specific conglomerate. It is the arrangement of the instruments within this conglomerate that will have a great effect upon the ultimate sound of the group. It is therefore necessary to make a decision as to how the instrumentation of the group is to be handled.

At one end of the philosophical scale is the "let the members play whatever instruments they want" theory. At the other end is the sounder idea that the band should be balanced with certain instruments in each family and sub-families.

Ratio of Woodwinds to Brass

The ratio of woodwinds to brass is an important factor in determining the type of sound a band produces. It is not the only factor, to be sure. The band director's concept of sound desired is perhaps almost as important as the ratio factor.

The ratio of the various types of instrumental groups breaks down in this manner:

symphonic band: ⅔ woodwinds, ⅓ brass
wind ensemble: nearly 50–50 but a few more woodwinds
military band: nearly 50–50 but a few more brass

Percussion instruments make up from 6% to 8% of all types of groups.

Ratio vs. Tone-Balance

Among the most important factors determining the tone-balance of a band is the ratio of woodwinds to brasses. Each individual conductor usually knows how he wants his band to sound. However, he must also consider the ability of the individual instrumentalists within the band, for they determine to a great extent the actual ratio that might be needed in certain situations to attain the quality desired.

When the clarinet section, for example, is covering a flute solo, reducing the number of clarinets by two or three or even four does not always help (unless it is a very small clarinet section). It is necessary to reduce the number in significant proportions to improve the situation (if this seems to be the only solution). There is, however, a difference between the quality of sound produced by a section of ten clarinets and that produced by a section containing 16 or 20. Though the dynamics may be reduced to a proper level in a large section when a number of instruments are asked not to play, the quality of sound will also be altered. Changing the numbers will (to some extent) change the dynamics, but it also changes the tone quality.

Dynamic levels do not change in direct proportion to the number of instruments. If, for example, five trombones produce a sound level of 50 decibels, adding two or more will probably raise the level to 51 or 52 decibels, not to 70, as simple arithmetic might lead one to conclude.

It is not possible to operate on the assumption that two plus two equals four when determining a proper balance for a band. The Weber-Fecher law states that sound increases in proportion to the logarithm of energy and not in proportion to the energy present. The sound energy produced by a trumpet playing a high C at 70 decibels is 10,000,000 units of sound energy. There would thus have to be 100 flutes to completely balance that one trumpet.

Concerning the ratio of woodwinds to brass, it would be possible with the proper shadings to perform most literature with a one-to-one ratio. The band's tone quality, however, dictates something more than this. Generally this means there should be one and absolutely no more than two to each part in the cornet and trumpet section. As for the baritones and trombones, two to a part is highly desirable. Woodwinds on the other hand (except for oboes and saxophones) require multiple performers on all the parts.

Symphonic vs. Concert vs. Wind Ensemble

The delineation between a symphonic and a concert band has not been conclusively established. However, one generally thinks of a symphonic band in terms of a symphonic orchestra—not so much that it only plays symphonies but that it is a very large organization containing the whole gamut of instruments available, including contrabassoon, double players on the winds, English horn, bass trombone, tuba, etc., built around a foundation of a very large string section, from the high violins to the double octave string bass. So, too, the symphonic band is a large ensemble containing all the instruments useful to it—contra-bassoon, double players on the cornets, trumpets and French horn parts, English horn, bass trombones, tubas, etc., built around a foundation of a very large clarinet section from the high E-flat to the double octave contrabass.

As a rule of thumb, after consulting some charts on instrumentation that appear later in this chapter, the concert band would be that organization containing up to 85 players. The symphonic band is that group containing 85 or more.

Since 1952, through the efforts of Frederick Fennell, the wind ensemble has become a very definite type of organization having the following instrumentation (21 woodwinds, 16 brass):

2 flutes and piccolos	3 cornets or 5 trumpets
2 oboes and English horn	2 trumpets
2 bassoons and contrabassoon	4 French horns
1 E-flat clarinet	3 trombones
8 B-flat clarinets	2 euphoniums
1 alto clarinet	2 tubas
1 bass clarinet	
2 alto saxophones	Percussion, harp, etc., as
1 tenor saxophone	needed
1 baritone saxophone	

The wind ensemble offers the conductor and players a different concept and approach to a fairly large performing group of mixed winds (beyond what is normally considered a small ensemble), from that of the symphonic or concert band.

As in small ensemble playing, the wind ensemble gives its members more individuality than that afforded those playing in a symphonic band. This is particularly true of those in large sections like the clarinet, trombone, or flute. This type of group can provide an outlet for the highly skilled players. It can challenge these persons beyond that level which would be possible in the concert band.

"Basic" Instrumentation for Concert/Symphonic Band

Three arranger-composers (Buchtel, Fred, Yoder) were asked by Traugott Rohner[1] to list a minimum basic instrumentation. All agreed on the following parts:

3 clarinets	2 trombones
3 cornet-trumpets	1 tuba
1 baritone	1 percussion

This, then, we might call "Basic Instrumentation No. 1."

To No. 1 the following can be added to give us "Basic Instrumentation No. 2."

2 flutes-piccolos
2 horns in F
2 saxophones (E-flat alto, E-flat baritone)

In an effort to establish some sort of standardization for evaluation purposes, in the January 1966 issue of *The Instrumentalist* I set down some typical instrumentations for various sized bands based upon available information. Thus was established the following numbers and proportions: [2]
Instrumentation for a band with 25 players—11 woodwinds, 12 brass:

1 flute	4 cornet-trumpets
1 oboe	3 French horns
1 bassoon	3 trombones
6 B-flat clarinets	1 baritone
1 alto saxophone	1 tuba
1 tenor saxophone	2 percussion

---

[1] Traugott Rohner, "The Small Band—Instrumentation Symposium," *The Instrumentalist,* VI, 5 (March-April, 1952), 15.

[2] Russell A. Pizer, "Criteria for Evaluating an Instrumental Music Department," *The Instrumentalist,* XX, 6 (January, 1966), 32.

For a 30 piece band—16 woodwinds, 12 brass:

2 flutes	4 cornet-trumpets
1 oboe	3 French horns
1 bassoon	3 trombones
10 B-flat clarinets	1 baritone
1 alto saxophone	1 tuba
1 tenor saxophone	2 percussion

For a 40 piece band—24 woodwinds, 14 brass:

4 flutes	4 cornet-trumpets
2 oboes	4 French horns
2 bassoons	3 trombones
10 B-flat clarinets	1 baritone
2 alto clarinets	2 tubas
1 bass clarinet	3 percussion
2 alto saxophones	
1 tenor saxophone	

For a 50 piece band—28 woodwinds, 18 brass:

6 flutes	4 cornets
2 oboes	2 trumpets
2 bassoons	4 French horns
10 B-flat clarinets	3 trombones
2 alto clarinets	1 bass trombone
2 bass clarinets	2 baritones
2 alto saxophones	2 tubas
1 tenor saxophone	4 percussion
1 baritone saxophone	

For a 65 piece band—38 woodwinds, 23 brass:

6 flutes	4 cornets
2 bassoons	2 trumpets
3 oboes	6 French horns
14 B-flat clarinets	4 trombones
4 alto clarinets	1 bass trombone
4 bass clarinets	3 baritones
1 contrabass clarinet	3 tubas
2 alto saxophones	4 percussion
1 tenor saxophone	
1 baritone saxophone	

For an 85 piece band—49 woodwinds, 30 brass:

6 flutes	6 cornets
3 oboes	4 trumpets
4 bassoons	6 French horns
1 E-flat clarinet	4 trombones
22 B-flat clarinets	2 bass trombones
4 alto clarinets	4 baritones
4 bass clarinets	4 tubas
1 contrabass clarinet	6 percussion
2 alto saxophones	
1 tenor saxophone	
1 baritone saxophone	

For a 100 piece band—58 woodwinds, 36 brass:

10 flutes	6 cornets
3 oboes	4 trumpets
4 bassoons	8 French horns
1 E-flat clarinet	6 trombones
24 B-flat clarinets	2 bass trombones
4 alto clarinets	4 baritones
4 bass clarinets	6 tubas
2 contrabass clarinets	6 percussion
4 alto saxophones	
1 tenor saxophone	
1 baritone saxophone	

Maintaining Consistent Instrumentation

Maintaining consistent instrumentation is a process that begins in the lower grades and continues through high school. In the lower grades there should be frequent references to the need for a balanced instrumentation whenever the band director talks to his various groups about the band and how it should sound.

The Instrumentation Taxonomy (Illustration 1-1) may be of aid in seeking a solution to this problem. This chart can be used in three ways. First, the band director can use it to lay out the number of students he has, compare that against the number

INSTRUMENTATION TAXONOMY

for _____

	THOSE LEAVING	TOTALS NEEDED	THOSE REMAINING 11th	THOSE REMAINING 12th	THOSE COMING	PROJECTED NEEDS	# TO TRANS. OUT
FLUTE	3	6	1	2	5	3	2
OBOE	1	3	0	1	0	1	
BASSOON	1	2	0	1	0		
Bb CLARINET	2	14	6	4	8	4	4
ALTO CLARINET		4					
BASS CLARINET		4					
CONTRABASS CL.		1					
ALTO SAXOPHONE		2					
TENOR SAXOPHONE		1					
BARI. SAXOPHONE		4					
CORNET		4					
TRUMPET		2					
FRENCH HORN		6					
TROMBONE		4					
BASS TROMBONE		1					
BARITONE		3					
TUBA		3					
PERCUSSION		4					

ETC.

TOTAL ____ 65

NOTE: The numbers placed in the boxes are just some examples of how to figure the taxonomy.

ILLUSTRATION 1-1

graduating and the number coming in from the junior high school; and compare it to the number he desires to have in each section to achieve a balance. Second, this chart could be posted on the band's bulletin board a month before school is out in the spring. During the last few rehearsals some time could be spent discussing the needs the band will have for September. In this way some students may even voluntarily come forth "for the good of the band" to transfer to other instruments that may be needed for this balance. Third, this chart could be mimeographed and presented to the members of the band parents club. After a few years of discussing this problem the parents will come to grips with it and assist the director in pursuading their own children to volunteer to aid the band in achieving this needed balance.

Illustration 1-2 (Transfers from . . . . to . . . .) could also be posted on the bulletin board or duplicated and given to the parents so they can see to what instrument one might most easily be transferred.

Some sort of talk or method of persuasion may be needed to convince the members of the band and their parents that these transfers are indeed necessary and are not just a whim of the band director.

One arguing point could be a comparison with the Physical Education Department. The band is constantly being associated with their marching band and basketball pep band.

Just as the coach on the football or basketball team decides which boys play which part, so too the band director must take this prerogative if there are not sufficient numbers of instruments in any given section. Every boy on the football team cannot be the right end that goes for the long, winning pass. Some have to be guards; some have to be tackles. In the same way all those in the band cannot be the first cornetist or clarinetist. We have to have bass clarinets and tubas. Just as the guard and tackle are the foundation from which the end works, so too the bass

TRANSFERS CAN BE MADE FROM . . . . to . . . .

WOODWINDS

FROM:	flute	Bb clarinet	saxophone
TO:	oboe bassoon saxophone alto clarinet bass clarinet	bassoon alto clarinet bass clarinet contrabass cl. saxophone	other saxophones bassoon alto clarinet bass clarinet contrabass cl. oboe

BRASS

FROM:	cornet-trumpet	baritone	trombone
TO:	French horn baritone tuba trombone	tuba trombone	baritone tuba

ILLUSTRATION 1-2

clarinet players and tuba players are the men upon which the melody for the clarinet and cornet are built.

This might be pointed out rather clearly by presenting a chart of the various instrumentations for different sizes of bands. Explain to the group that this is what constitutes a band of, for example, 65 pieces. It calls for 14 B-flat clarinets. We can add a few more but *only* after all the other parts are adequately covered. We need four alto clarinets, four bass clarinets and one contrabass to balance a section of 14 B-flat clarinets. Now, if we had the four altos, four basses and a contrabass, this group could support up to as many as 20 B-flat clarinets. But we have to get the lower instruments before adding on to the top.

It is true that there are some buildings being built today whose upper stories stick out beyond the lower ones, but even here there is a limit to how far out they can go. The band is a little like that. We have a B-flat clarinet section upon which hangs the bottom or foundation of the band. However, this foundation, like that of a building, cannot be too small.

The importance of balance could be graphically illustrated by taking an old full score and completely blacking out the contrabass clarinet part, the second horn part, a bassoon part, or some other such combination which might be missing for the next semester. Then explain that it is true that the average listener cannot hear when this part is not being adequately covered. But if the band is entering a contest, it is especially important that these instruments be provided because the judge just might expect to hear them, and if he does not the band could be penalized.

Some additional incentives can be offered to band members if they switch to a needed instrument. If the band uses a point system for awards and the giving of grades, those switching would be given some extra points—with most points given to the least desirable instruments.

Because it is necessary that some training be given to those transferring, those willing to do this could be given, for incentive purposes, a semester of free private lessons on that instrument.

Just in case the question arises: there is no necessity for a parent to purchase an instrument since the needed ones are usually the larger ones provided by the school.

So that the student and his parents do not feel that he is stuck with the instrument for life, the policy should be that the transfer is for the concert and contest season only. At the end of that time the student may go back to his own instrument if he so desires.

If there are some members of the band who plan to go on to study music in college this could be used as a means of persuasion. Since they will have to learn to play most of the instruments, they might as well get a head start here in high school.

Because of the additional costs that would be involved in the purchase of reeds for the bassoon, the alto, bass and contrabass clarinets, as well as the baritone saxophone, the school might provide these free to the transferring students. Whenever this is done, however, many students become careless with these "free gifts." If they had to pay out their own money they might not be so careless.

two

Working Out Effective Sections and Seating Arrangements

Regardless of the amount of pre-planning that goes into the choice of instrumentation, there are bound to be variances from year to year in the strengths and weaknesses of individual players and sections. Given this ever-changing situation it is necessary to make the best use of the instruments and players that are available. Altering seating arrangements, changing sizes of sections or placing sections in different locations can contribute to the improvement of the overall sound. While careful selection of music (to be discussed in Chapter 7) is a most important factor in the production of a good-sounding band, this chapter is devoted to the effects of sectional balance and seating arrangements.

How to Arrange the Woodwinds

No matter what size the band may be, one piccolo is usually sufficient. Though not listed on most instrumentation charts it is taken for granted that the first flutist doubles on the piccolo whenever it is needed. It is conceivable that for special occasions more than one might be used, as in the trio of the "Stars and Stripes Forever." These instruments, because they are so small, are very difficult to play in tune with themselves. The problems are compounded if two or three are used. The tone of one piccolo is sufficiently brilliant so that it will stand out above the band when used.

One oboe to a part is usually adequate for any size band. The difficulties of intonation and blend make doubling this instrument hazardous. In larger bands a third oboe is added, but its primary purpose is to play the English horn parts whenever necessary. When no English horn parts are written, this third person usually doubles the second oboe part provided the first oboist is sufficiently strong to carry off his part alone.

As there are two bassoon parts, two instruments are usually sufficient. Their parts in the larger bands can be doubled with good effect. The bassoon's tone is such that it is easily covered by other instruments, so more power may be desirable in this section. In a very large band a contrabassoon added to the section would give great depth to the double reed section. This instrument could double the second bassoon parts when feasible, giving a lower octave sonority that is very fine sounding.

Improving the Clarinet Section

The clarinet choir within the symphonic band is the foundation upon which the high degree of sonority or the degree of brilliance is achieved. In the symphonic type organization where a large clarinet section is used, a dark, rich sonority may be achieved. The lack of great numbers of clarinets and the increased numbers of brass—particularly trumpets—is what gives the band the "military" sound, i.e., greater brilliance.

A bright, brilliant edge can be added to the rich clarinet sonority through the use of the piccolo and the E-flat soprano clarinet. Also, the E-flat clarinet can play some parts with better intonation than the B-flat soprano in the extreme upper range.

As with the piccolo, there is little need for more than one E-flat soprano clarinet in almost any size band. The brilliance of only one is usually sufficient to sound above the rest of the clarinet choir whenever it is played by a good strong person. Another reason for using only one is that in general it is difficult to play in tune. Though this is usually blamed on the instrument itself, a player with a good sense of intonation should have little trouble with it. If a greater degree of brilliance is desired it is conceivable that more than one could be used—but only if used judiciously.

The B-flat clarinet section is usually divided into three parts— solo or first, second and third. There are occasional arrangements, notably of European origin, that call for four parts—either solo, first, second and third or first, second, third and fourth.

The numbers used on each part vary greatly, depending upon the size of the section. Generally, however, the greater number are placed on the second and third parts. If the band contains nine clarinets there would conceivably be three on a part. When the number rises to ten, there would probably be three placed on first, three on second and four on third. If one were to follow the instrumentation stated previously for a 40-piece band where nine clarinets and two altos are used, the combination could be three firsts, four seconds, and two thirds. The alto clarinet which usually doubles the third clarinet part would make up for the two third clarinets and actually give better balance than 3, 3, 3. In a band where there are ten clarinets the relative numbers might be three firsts, four seconds, and three thirds, again relying upon the alto clarinets to add to the third clarinet's sound.

In bands containing 14 clarinets, there would still be fewer placed on the first part—perhaps four, six on the second and four on the third—again depending upon the alto clarinets. In a band of 24 clarinets the ratio might be four firsts, ten seconds and ten thirds. If the thirds are sufficiently strong (with the added tone of the alto clarinets) and if, during rehearsals, the seconds are not coming through in proper balance, the proportions might be switched to 4, 12 and 8.

The use of fewer clarinets on the first part is for two reasons: first, this part is generally high and will naturally sound out;

secondly, the better and stronger players in the band are placed on the first part. Another reason for using fewer on the first part is because of intonation problems. The extremely high notes they often play are difficult to play in tune, and by adding additional numbers, the band director has added intonation problems.

Some feel that the alto clarinet does not add enough to the overall sound of the band to warrant the expense necessary to purchase the instrument. It is true that the alto clarinet can have a somewhat hollow and nasal sound, but if played properly it can and should be sonorous and mellow.

It is of the greatest importance that at least two be introduced into the band at the same time. One alto clarinet will most certainly be lost in the total band sound and will thus be of little value. This is not entirely the instrument's fault, however. One reason this situation exists is that rarely will a band director take one of his strong players and place him on this instrument. It is therefore advantageous to have two, each giving the other confidence and each sharing in the same musical problems.

It is extremely important that students who switch to the alto clarinet be taught to play it correctly, especially if they had been playing B-flat soprano clarinet. Too often a student switching from the B-flat soprano merely thinks of the alto as just another B-flat soprano and does not compensate for its larger bore, increased length, larger mouthpiece, different angle and bite.

The alto clarinet can add resonance in tonal colorings to the band. Its lower register blends well with the top register of the bass clarinet, giving more sonority to the ensemble tone. It can also enrich the lower tones of the B-flat soprano clarinets. It is especially valuable in reinforcing the all-too-often weak third clarinet part.

The bass clarinet represents a rich tenor voice for the clarinet section of the band. Its depth of sound gives a rich, resonant tone, filling the gap between the low register or the B-flat soprano clarinet and the low bass tones of the tuba, though in some bands it fills the gap between the alto clarinet and the contrabass. Its use to the clarinet section is as important as the cello voice is to the string section of the orchestra. Its low tones act as a tonal enforcement of the overtones being produced by the entire clarinet section. Like the contrabass clarinet and the string bass, it cannot always be heard, but its tone would certainly be missed if it were to be deleted from an ensemble that is accustomed to its added resonance.

The contrabass clarinet, the most recent addition to the instrumentation of the band, fulfills the need for a truly bass voice for the clarinet section. Previously the only true bass available was the tuba. Some people found the use of the string bass aided in achieving a lighter or more delicate sound in the lower reaches of the musical scale. But on the whole, these two instruments were inadequate in providing the desired bass voice. The contrabassoon could partially fulfill this need but the extreme expense to the usually limited budget often rules it out. Also, its tone is not equal to the sonority of the rest of the clarinets which it is to support; it is too vibrant and reedy sounding. Though it is quite agile, its lower notes—those of greatest value—are not as easily playable as are the lower notes on an instrument like the clarinet. The tuba's tone quality is too different to be blended into a portion of a composition for the clarinet section. It also seriously lacks sufficient agility, except in the hands of a highly skilled performer, to fill the post of the bass of the clarinet section.

There are actually two contrabass clarinets: an E-flat contra-alto and a B-flat contrabass. The choice of which one to use may simply come down to a convenience factor.

Because there are many compositions that do not have parts written for the contrabass it is necessary for the band director either to write a special part or adapt a part from another instrument. The B-flat contrabass requires a transposed part but the E-flat contra-alto does not. The E-flat player can merely add three sharps to the key signature of any written part for a bass clef instrument. He then merely reads the part as if it were in treble clef. The contra-alto player can thus read any existing bass clef part easily. For example: if the bass clef part contains three flats, the added three sharps cancel the three flats so the student merely plays the part in the key of *C*. Likewise, if the part contains two flats, two of the flats are canceled by two of the sharps with one left over. The left-over sharp then becomes the key signature—the key of *G*.

Alfred Reed and James Neilson [1] have set down eight uses to which the contrabass clarinet can be put:

1. double or substitute for Bassoon II line parts in lower registers when it is obvious that composers and arrangers thought the bassoon to be the only low woodwind available for this purpose,

2. use to double or substitute for the E-flat baritone saxophone when this instrument provides the only bass line, especially when it is obvious that the composer or arranger has been handicapped in providing a bass line part moving in the right direction due to the baritone's limited lower range,

3. may be used to double the string bass when the string bass alone provides the bass line part. At this time only the contrabass clarinet can successfully reinforce the string bass tone.

4. may be used as a double and thus give percussive impact to string bass pizzicati scored for tubas alone in transcriptions from the orchestral repertory, a most effective doubling,

5. together with the bass clarinet, the contrabass clarinet may double, or substitute for an octave bass line part given to baritone and tuba in softer brass passages when the important melody is in the French horn, or in softer passages which are predominantly woodwind and French horn in their sonority. This kind of scoring adds an intensly rich sonority to these softer passages, so much so that it may be necessary to reduce the number of baritones and tubas to one each, or perhaps

---

[1] Alfred Reed and James Neilson, *Scoring for the Contra-Alto and Contrabass Clarinet* (Kenosha, Wisconsin: G. Leblanc Corp., 1964), p. 2.

eliminate them entirely in order to avoid overbalancing the instruments playing above the bass line. This use of the bass and contrabass clarinets invariably results in a better blend and almost unbelievable refinement of ensemble sonority.

6. may be used as an effective double on virtuoso tuba parts (mostly transcribed string bass parts from the orchestral repertory) which make undue technical demands on bass players. The technical dexterity of the instrument, the sharp clarity of its staccato attack or smooth-flowing quality of its fast legato, even in the hands of less-experienced performers, make it ideally suited to this use, and always astonish those who have heard the contrabass clarinet playing nothing other than sustained tones or the usual "oom-pah" patterns.

7. may be used to double the bass trombone and give additional acoustical sheen to softer brass choir passages when only the bass trombone has a bass line part,

8. together with other mellow-voiced low woodwinds, the contrabass clarinet may be used to double or substitute for tubas in all softer passages of transcribed orchestral music originally scored for strings alone, especially in slow movements of symphonies or concerti.

Controlling the Saxophones

The saxophone section of the band is universally accepted to be a quartet—two altos, a first and a second, one tenor and one baritone. The combination seems to be sufficient to carry off the normal duties which are assigned the section. Occasionally a B-flat soprano part may be called for, but this is usually substituted in place of the first alto part as this person merely doubles on that instrument whenever it is called for.

Because of the conical bore of these instruments their projection is not a great problem unless the section is overloaded with doubling all the parts. In a band of 100 or more it does become necessary to double the parts, but this is usually only done for the alto parts, so there are two first altos, two second altos, one tenor and one baritone. Any more doubling than this produces a preponderance of sound that is difficult to manage and blend into the total sound picture. A particular problem created by multiple saxophones is that they tend to "rob" the French horn section of its sound.

Part of the problem with the saxophones arises because many people think of the saxophone as being one of the easiest instruments to play. In many ways it is, but in the most crucial—intonation—it is far from easy. This problem is usually compounded because often those who are relegated to playing the tenor or baritone are weaker clarinetists. As a result they do not approach the instrument with the seriousness they might if they were playing in the first clarinet section. The results become apparent because the tenor ends up being played with a very weak tone and the baritone is a honky monster that usually blats out its lower notes even on soft passages.

To solve the excessive doubling problem, some school systems do not teach saxophone in the feeder programs. A student can transfer to saxophone only when he has successfully played clarinet for a number of years and has a good sense of pitch and some sensitivity in playing.

Balancing the Brass Section

Most parts for the brass section consist of three separate cornet parts, two separate trumpet parts, four French horn parts, three trombone parts, one baritone and one tuba part.

The following chart by William A. Schaffer [2] suggests workable proportions between the voices of brass choirs of various sizes. It will be noted that top parts are doubled in the smaller units, in recognition of the problem of endurance in performance, but that in larger sections the greater doubling tends toward the lower parts of sections.

2 William A. Schaffer, "The Brass Choir in the Band," *The Instrumentalist,* XX, 2 (September, 1965), 52.

Cornet I	2	2	2	2	2	2
Cornet II	1	1	2	2	3	4
Cornet III	1	2	2	2	3	4
Trumpet I	(1)	1	1	2	2	2
Trumpet II	(1)	1	1	2	2	2
Horn I	1	2	2	2	2	3
Horn II	1	1	2	2	3	3
Horn III	1	1	1	2	2	3
Horn IV	(1)	1	2	2	3	3
Trombone I	1	1	2	2	3	3
Trombone II	1	1	2	2	3	3
Trombone III	1	2	2	3	3	4
Baritone	1	2	2	3	3	3
Tuba	1	2	2	3	3	4

Balancing the Cornets and Trumpets

Generally in smaller bands the directors have a tendency to interchange the cornets and trumpets without regard to the fact that these are separate and distinctly different instruments. This interchange, to be sure, is more out of necessity than desire. If the best player in the band happens to have a trumpet he will be placed on the part that calls for the most work in the rendering of a composition. This most often is designated as a first cornet part. Placing a weaker player, merely because he owns a cornet, on this first part is not a very logical or wise decision.

When determining the type of sound one wishes to create in his band, besides the ratio of woodwinds to brass, the use of trumpets in relation to the use of cornets is a big factor. For those who desire a bright, military-type sound the use of trumpets on the major parts will give the desired effect. If one desires a more rich or mellow sound from his band, cornets should be used in the ratios given in the previous chart.

Vincent Bach, a leading authority on brass instruments, wrote the following about the "trumpet vs. cornet:"

"There are no arbitrary laws regarding the construction of

cornets and trumpets, and various manufacturers use different proportions for these two instruments. Bach trumpets are 50% cylindrical bore and 50% conical bore, while our cornet is about 90% conical and only 10% cylindrical. If used on open tones, the trumpet has one winding and the cornet has two windings of tubing.

"The trumpet tone is not so flexible as that of a cornet and it is more difficult to slur from one note to another—which is of good advantage when playing a fortissimo attack. The cornet, with the more conical bore and two windings, produces greater resistance. This allows a better diction, causes the tone to be more flexible, and makes it possible for the player to slur from one note to the other more easily. It is, therefore, better suited to coloratura work. By the same token, however, one can more easily slip off a note. The cornet is not well suited to fanfare or staccato playing.

"A small bore will produce a more brilliant tone than a large bore. If you compare a small bore cornet with a large bore trumpet, the trumpet will have a more mellow tone, and vice versa. Instruments made by different manufacturers have different bell tapers, so you cannot draw a general conclusion by comparing a cornet of one make with a trumpet of another make. When talking about easy playing, you also have to answer the question: What is easy—the staccato, or the legato, or the dynamics? Remember that neither instrument will produce anything that you don't blow into it." [3]

Acton Ostling, Jr., sets forth some other arguments in this controversy:

"Accounts of various 'behind a screen' tests in which a difference between the cornet and trumpet was inaudible to the listeners are numerous, and can be quoted *ad infinitum* by the

---

[3] Vincent Bach, "Know Your Brasses," *Selmer Bandwagon*, XV, 1 (April, 1967), 13.

'orchestral' bandsmen. It is impossible to imagine such tests conducted with two genuine styles of playing since the person who performs *both* styles well is more than a rarity. There are trumpet players who sound like cornetists, and vice versa. Given two performers, with each player musically coversant in a different style, one with a *true* cornet and the other with an orchestral trumpet, playing *typical* parts for each instrument, the difference *will* be noticeable." [4]

The French Horn

Because composers and arrangers are not always certain that bands will contain at least four French horns, it is a common practice to write the more important tones of the chord for the first and second horns. The third most important tone in the chord is then given to the third horn. The fourth horn then simply doubles one of the other tones being played by another horn if it is a three-tone chord. This situation leads to the practice whereby the third horn part most often lies higher in range than the second. It is therefore a customary practice to place the horn players with the best high ranges on the first and third parts and the horn players with the good lower ranges on the second and fourth parts. Horn players are thus not seated or assigned parts as are those in other sections. The actual technical ability is often secondary to ability to play well in various registers.

The Bass Trombone

The third trombone part in most band compositions is doubled in at least one and in some cases several other parts. In marches, for example, the third trombone part is often exactly the same as

---

[4] Action Ostling, Jr., "Why Not Cornets and Trumpets?" *The Instrumentalist,* XXI, 11 (June, 1967), 37.

the E-flat tuba. The bass clarinet as well as the baritone saxophone part often closely resembles that of the third trombone. The range of the third trombone part rarely goes lower than the F immediately below the bass clef. This seems to indicate that there is no real need to purchase a bass trombone to play this part.

It is true that the tenor trombone can adequately cover this part. However, because of the larger bore of a real bass trombone (not just a tenor trombone with an F attachment), it is better suited to this low part. The bass trombone thus more effectively bridges the tonal difference between the smaller bore tenor trombone and the tuba.

Baritone vs. Euphonium

There is a difference between a baritone and a euphonium. The baritone is a small bore instrument while the euphonium has a large bore. It is for this reason that the euphonium's tone quality favors lower tones than does the true baritone. In Europe both instruments are used separately. European bands usually have different parts for these instruments—one for the baritone and another for the euphonium. The instrument used in America is a cross between the English baritone and the euphonium. Hence this instrument is called by either name while probably it would be more accurate to use both, i.e., a baritone-euphonium.

Sometimes the differentiation is made, incorrectly, depending upon the part written for it—a treble clef or bass clef part. Many band works are published with both a treble clef and a bass clef part but only for the director's convenience. Both parts are exactly the same, pitch-wise. The difference is that the treble clef part is written so that any cornet player, by using the cornet fingerings, can play the part on the euphonium; it is a transposed part written for a B-flat instrument. The bass clef part is a C part—non transposing. To play this part one has to adapt to a concert pitch fingering.

Sousaphone or Tuba?

Inevitably, the question of whether to use sousaphones, recording basses, or upright tubas arises. The sousaphone is still the most practical instrument for schools that cannot afford two sets of tubas. It is indispensable for the marching band and serves adequately in the concert band. However, wherever possible, the sousaphone is best replaced by either the upright or recording models for concert use.

While necessity often dictates whether or not to use sousaphones in the large ensemble, the question of upright or bell-front recording models is not so easily answered. This is determined only after considering the type of sound desired and the acoustics of the areas in which they are to be used. Generally speaking, the upright bell tends to give the instrument a brighter sound and a bit more clarity to the articulation. The bell-front models are obviously more directional and tend to have a more "spread" or less brilliant sound, and the articulation does not seem as crisp as it is on the upright tuba.

Along with determining the size of the section, deciding the type of instruments is equally important. In bands today the BBb tuba has become the most popular. This popularity has risen from the fact that it has an extensive low register while maintaining a high register that is adequate for playing the entire band repertoire.

Unfortunately, even though there are many of them available, the E-flat tuba has become relegated to the role of a beginner's instrument because it is smaller than the BBb and more easily handled. However, the E-flat tuba is not merely a beginner's instrument. One E-flat should be used in each section to double the BBb tubas one octave higher whenever possible. Because the E-flat tuba has a higher range than the BBb, it is much easier for the E-flat to articulate clearly in this register.

This one tuba playing an octave higher has a tendency to clear up and avoid the muddiness that often occurs in a section during the performance of passages lying in the lower register of the BBb tuba.

Improving the Sound of the Tuba Section

A good tuba section is one that can play a full rich legato bass line along with rhythmically accurate accompaniments.

Since the concert band deals with more than just one tuba some decision must be made in regard to how many to use. There must be enough tubas to provide a firm bass or bottom when the ensemble is playing at *fortissimo*, yet not so many as to cause a thick, logy sound or sloppy articulation. The difficulty arises because of the extreme length of tubing and the low pitch. Therefore it is more difficult for several tubas to play cleanly than for an equal number of clarinets or cornets. This is not to indicate in any way that good articulation in a tuba section is impossible. It is, however, often necessary to edit out a portion of a large tuba section from time to time for the sake of clarity. If a section should contain six tubas it may often be necessary to ask only three or even two to play in light *piano* passages. If the part is at the extreme bottom of the range it is helpful to have some play the part up an octave. In some cases the tuba section should be looked upon like the percussion—it is not necessary, just because you have all those instruments, to use them all of the time.

The String Bass

Concerning the string bass in the band, Frank Hill writes the following: [5] "Formerly the string bass was needed in the band to replace the tuba in areas of the music that called for lightness like the accompaniment of a single flute line accompanied by the

---

[5] Frank Hill, "The String Bass in Bands," *The Instrumentalist*, XVII, 7 (March, 1963), 56.

clarinet section. The contrabass clarinet now takes over this task. Even with the use of the contrabass clarinet, Mark Hindsley feels: 'The deep bass of the clarinet choir should be provided by contrabass clarinets, supplemented by string basses. If string basses are available, the E-flat contrabass clarinet would receive first preference over the BBb instrument. The contrabass clarinets and the string basses should be considered as one section serving as the bottom not only of the clarinets, but also the complete woodwind choir. In addition to its other qualities, the string bass pizzicato is invaluable. With the low bass voice of woodwinds and strings the brass basses may be used more sparingly in delicate spots.' "

Variety in Your Percussion Section

The need for a great variety of percussion instruments is growing steadily. Their addition to the band is no longer only one of rhythmic impulse but is actually contributing in many cases to the timbre of the overall sound. In order to cover the minimum requirements called for in most symphonic arrangements there should be at least five players. The most common instruments called for include snare drum, bass drum, cymbals (crash and suspended), tympani, and a variety of traps such as triangle, wood blocks, gong, bells, etc.

The number of percussion instruments a band should have might be stated like this: as many as the band's budget will allow. How and when and which ones are acquired is often determined by the needs of the moment. It is necessary, however, to build up a large inventory of these instruments through long range purchasing.

How to Arrange Seating for Maximal Effectiveness

There are almost as many seating arrangements as there are bands. However, there are seven fundamental principles upon which seating is based. It will often be found that even though one desires a particular seating plan the exact location of instruments is determined more by the facilities, i.e., the rehearsal room or the concert stage, than by the individual's desires.

Whenever possible, and whichever combination proves to be the most advantageous, one should:

1. seat all players in such a way that they can see the conductor —a must!
2. seat like instruments together;
3. seat large sections in a block;
4. seat instruments playing the same parts in close proximity;
5. seat persons playing first parts in close proximity;
6. place instruments so their tone is presented in its most advantageous manner;
7. place instruments neither where their projection over-burdens the total balance of the group nor in such a place that they must force their tone to be heard.

These principles cannot all be followed, and in some cases, as will be seen, should not be followed to the letter.

The first principle may seem obvious, but the director should keep a wary eye out for those in his band who cannot possibly watch him because of the way they are positioned. It is difficult enough to get all band members to watch the conductor without having the added problem of a chair positioned so that a student is facing in the direction of the fourth trombone or something equally bad. Most times a problem of this sort arises because of improper placement of the music stand. The stand must be placed on a line between the player's eyes and the director. Having two bandsmen read off one stand does create somewhat of a problem. Those on the stand must make adjustments and compromise this straight line direction so that each has a vision line somewhat in the direction of the conductor. At no time should three be allowed to read from one stand. Making adjustments so that all three can see the director is practically impossible; besides, the outside players will have to be a long way from the score and will have difficulty reading it. When the larger instruments are concerned, especially tubas, only one should be allowed to a stand. Even in the case of the percussion, the snare drummer should not have to look over to the bass drummer's stand or vice versa.

The height of the music stand is also important. It should be adjusted so that the middle of the musical score is on a level with the player's eyes. In this way, if the conductor uses a podium, the player can look at his score and see the conductor at the same time. The eye's field of vision is sufficient so that the player will see the conductor even if he does not seem to be looking. Having the stand at the proper height not only contributes to the student's ability to watch the conductor, it also contributes to good posture. If the stand is kept too low, the posture will be poor because the student will have a tendency to slouch or bend over forward. Thus the player's eyes will be directed downward toward the floor, and in the case of instruments like the trombone, cornet and trumpet, their bells will also be pointed toward the floor, muted behind the stands and those people sitting in front of them rather than projected out toward the audience.

A band seating chart has three large blocks—the woodwinds at the front part of the organization, the brass toward the back, and the percussion at the far rear or on one of the far sides. The position of each group of instruments within these blocks can have an effect upon the total sound of the group. Certain seatings can give the band a more brilliant sound than others.

Seating like instruments together needs little explanation except to comment upon the seating within a group of like instruments. With instruments that are strung out in a single row, as the French horns usually are, it is well to place the weaker players so they surround the stronger ones. In this case, the section could be seated with the first horns toward the center of the row and the thirds and fourths on the outside. Seating a section in this fashion means that the last chair fourth player has only three chairs between himself and the first chair player. If they are seated in a chronological row the last chair would have six players in between (if the section contains eight horns).

This type of seating can also be of advantage when seating the tubas and even the cornets. This idea could also be carried over into the trombone, flute and clarinet sections, though it is rarely done because this principle will conflict too greatly with the fifth principle, which may be more important.

The exact position of each instrument within the woodwind section varies from band to band and is often determined by the players themselves. Some writers on the subject suggest that because of the way the flute sound projects it is best that they be seated to the left of the conductor. If there are six or eight flutes there should be two rows. Some suggest that the alto clarinet, bass clarinet and bassoons be seated in the second and third rows, in front of the conductor. The low woodwind sound characteristic of the symphonic band is then incorporated into the heart of the band.

The oboes and bassoons are often placed in a location comparable to their position in the orchestra, i.e., directly in front of the conductor. This often is not a good place for the bassoons, however, because of their projection problems. Placing them on the outside at the conductor's right may allow for better projection possibilities—they will not be buried in the band and their instruments will be facing the audience. Though the projection of the oboes is not usually a problem they too could be placed out on the right side if more projection is needed.

The saxophone section's position is fairly well established on the right side of the band, usually in the second or third row. Again, if the section's sound is not as strong as the conductor desires, they can be placed on the outside right just in front of where the trombones might be seated.

Seating the Right Side

The right side varies greatly. Conceding that the first row to the right contains the flutes, the second row and third row vary widely. The last row usually is given to the trombones. Some of the various combinations might be:

2nd row: a good place for the saxophone section—alto on the outside, tenor and the fourth in—baritone. If the bassoons and oboes are placed in the second row center this would mean that the bassoons and the lower saxophones, who often play similar parts, will be in close proximity, in keeping with principle number 4.

3rd row: a good place for the low clarinets—altos on the outside, basses next and the contrabass furthest in. In a setup of this kind we have all the lower woodwinds in close proximity, directly in front of the lower brass sounds—the trombones and euphoniums.

If there is not sufficient room, the row immediately behind the flutes could be given to the alto, next row to the bass, next row to the saxophone section.

Having the alto clarinets on the outside right is a long way from the third clarinets, to be sure. As these instruments play very similar and many times directly duplicate parts one should place them on the other side with the third B-flat clarinets. The alto clarinets should be placed over by the third B-flat clarinets if either section, thirds or altos happen to be weak, for these then would tend to reinforce each other. Moving the alto clarinets over to the left would then advantageously place the bass clarinets out on the side where they will be better heard.

The internal arrangement of the B-flat clarinet section usually seats the best players on the first part, the worst players on the last, the average players on the second. Too often this makes for a strong first clarinet section, a weaker second and a very weak third. Though other arrangements occur infrequently there are some alternatives to this chronological seating, as will be seen on the next three charts.

Illustration 2-1 shows the position that bands normally have— best player first, second best player second, etc., with the weakest player last.

16	10	
15	9	
14	8	4
13	7	3
12	6	2
11	5	1

CONDUCTOR

ILLUSTRATION 2-1

Illustration 2-2 would appear ideal because the outside chair players of each section would be very strong and proficient. This would, however, place a much weaker player in the second chair position. This might cause great problems both in intonation and the technical dexterity often called for by the first clarinet parts. Illustration 2-3 might be a solution to this. In this setup the four best players are assigned to the first clarinet parts, then the remainder of the section is evenly divided among the better players in those two remaining sections.

The position of the French horns is fairly well standardized. They are usually placed directly in front of the conductor in the second or third row, depending upon how many flutes there are or whether the oboes and bassoons are placed in the center.

16	15	
14	13	
12	11	10
9	8	7
6	5	4
3	2	1

ILLUSTRATION 2-2

16	15	
14	13	
12	11	4
10	9	3
8	7	2
6	5	1

ILLUSTRATION 2-3

If the French horn section is not projecting sufficiently to meet the desires of the conductor, the first solution would be to place them on risers. Moving them so their bells face the audience is difficult because the clarinet section would be in the way. It would be possible to have only a few clarinets, say four, in the row with the horns, then they could be moved further around to the right. This would make for a little more projection. Having the horn bells facing the audience, however, is not too good because it would present a more brilliant sound than would normally be desired.

As for the other brasses, many conductors advocate their bells being placed so they blow directly at the audience to get the full value of their tone's projection. This would mean that behind the horns would be the cornets and trumpets, behind them the trombones, and one further row for the tubas and baritones. As most halls are not sufficiently deep to accommodate this type of setup, modifications must be necessary.

It is generally conceded that the baritones and tubas should be placed at the back of the band, somewhat together. The compromise comes between the trombone and cornet-trumpet sections. One of these groups will of necessity be placed on the right of the conductor in a row behind whatever woodwinds are there—probably in a large band in the fourth row.

The decision as to which instruments are to be facing the audience directly will be determined by the relative strength of both sections and the conductor's tone-concept desires. In a band with a large, strong cornet section, these could be placed on the outside right, fourth row. Placing them in this location would produce two effects. First, it would mean they were not blowing directly at the audience, thus softening to some extent the mass of sound they would produce. Second, the sounds that come off the side of the cornet-trumpet bell is more mellow, or less penetrating, than those that come directly out of the bore, thus giving a more mellow sound to the section.

Placing the trombones directly in front of the tubas in the center back gives a great deal of projection to these instruments—this important, and often lost, upper bass-tenor voice.

In general, one could say that the seating arrangement of a band is that which will make the band sound best (in the conductor's estimation) in keeping with his tone-balance concepts. It also means that once a seating arrangement is decided upon by the conductor it may not be used year after year. It will be changed to meet the needs, the strengths and the weaknesses of the various sections so that the band's best foot will be put forward.

three

Using Band Rehearsals
to Best Advantage

To paraphrase Shakespeare: what a rehearsal is and what it is not is an exceedingly important question.

What a rehearsal *is* will be discussed at length. To begin, however, it might be advantageous to state some things that a rehearsal *is not:*

A rehearsal is not a social hour. It is not a sight-reading session (though this is an important part of a rehearsal if properly scheduled). It is not the time to pass out music. It is not a concert for some mysteriously missing audience. It is not a time for self-congratulations and it is not a time to discipline individuals for past trangressions.

A rehearsal is a bringing together of the talents and under-standings of a group of individuals for the purpose of ultimately rendering a nearly perfect work of musical art subject only to the limitations of the individuals and the artistic interpretation of the conductor.

Creating a Productive Attitude

It has been said that the rehearsal is the price one has to pay for the privilege of participating in a performing art. Whether the rehearsal is regarded as a painful, tedious bore or as a giving of oneself to achieve a greater goal in a combined effort is principally a matter of attitude. The sacrifice of time and personal feelings is embodied in the true spirit of democratic ensemble. Rehearsing is working together while still accepting individual responsibility within a group.

In acknowledging that rehearsals can be painful, this quote from Kahil Gibran's book, *The Prophet,* seems appropriate: "Your pain is the breaking of the shell that encloses your understanding. Even as the stone of the fruit must break, that its heart may stand in the sun, so must you know pain. And could you keep your heart in wonder at the daily miracles of your life, your pain would not seem less wondrous than your joy."

Playing in a concert band involves some self-sacrifice. What better way for a student to learn that the giving of oneself is something each of us must learn eventually if we are to get the most out of life.

Quoting further from *The Prophet:* "You give but little when you give of your possessions. It is when you give of yourself that you truly give." The rehearsal can be made less painful if everyone will give of himself and make every rehearsal a performance in understanding.

The Nine Rehearsal Procedures

The rehearsal period is a combination of nine different procedural items. These items are somewhat interchangeable—some may be combined; some may be deleted from time to time or dropped altogether; some may receive more emphasis at different times of the year—all depending upon the band's total program, and upcoming events. These procedural items include:

1. rehearsal hall preparation
2. tune-up
3. warm-up
4. technical drill

5. familiar materials
6. rehearsal proper
7. sight reading
8. familiar pieces
9. announcements

Pre-planning the Rehearsal

Pre-planning does not mean only the few minutes before the bell rings and before the students begin moving into the rehearsal room. It includes the weeks and sometimes months of living with the musical scores of those works to be presented at the next public performance. It includes such things as research into the background of the compositions and composers and assimilating the information accumulated into a form for presentation to the band members. It might mean analyzing the chordal structure of a composition for the band members so they can better understand what is happening.

Though it may not be absolutely necessary for the band director to make out some sort of lesson plan for each rehearsal, it is important for him to know in advance just what items are to be covered in the rehearsal. Spending as little as five minutes before the rehearsal may be all that is needed, if only to decide in which order the compositions are going to be worked over.

The amount of planning put into the exact procedures for the rehearsal may well determine the extent to which the students in the organization are given a true "music education." Simply stepping to the front of the band and pulling a tune out of the folder to "run through" is not a truly professional approach to the task. There should be a definite plan of attack for the various items in the aforementioned procedures. Some questions that must be asked before the rehearsal begins would include: What procedure will be used today to warm up the band? Too often it is just playing through the B-flat scale again, and again, and again, and again. What about technical drill? If there is going to be some of this, what page or pages, and for what purpose or to what ends? Do you repeat what the band played yesterday, and the day before that and the day before that until they learn it? What about the rehearsal proper? Will there be some highly concentrated work on the major composition for the next concert or the contest number? Or is this to be a "play-through" day again?

Illustration 3-1 is a form that could be used as a planning guide for rehearsals. It is not too unlike that which most school districts expect of their classroom teachers. Most school teacher contracts require that lesson plans be made out. Some schools require long-range as well as day-to-day plans. Using a form like this would allow the director to lay out a scheme for playing through all the scales; for using different approaches to the warm-up procedure (like those to be discussed in Chapter 4); for using different approaches to the tuning process (like those to be discussed in Chapter 6), etc.

Preparing the Score

Studying the score is one of the most important parts of the pre-planning process. It has often been said that a conductor must not get in front of the group to conduct until he knows the score. Whereas no one will argue with this fact, the busy band director has little time to study each score thoroughly before bringing it to the band. Among the many writings on the subject of score studying is a fine work by James Neilson and Karl Holvik. Published by G. Leblanc Corporation, this ten-page booklet entitled "Studying the Full Score" suggests the following:

   I. Seek out and sing every melody, melodic counter-point and countrapuntal arc in the score.
  II. Analyze the harmonic background of all melodies and relate this to the phrase structure.
 III. Pencil the phrase structure in the score and mark the breathing places.

REHEARSAL PLANNING FORM

Date _____

Warm-up	Warm-up procedure

Tuning procedure	Special drill

Technical/musical discussions

Announcements

Composition	Work Needed/Procedures/ Pages/Measures/Etc.

ILLUSTRATION 3-1

IV. Analyze the rhythmic structure of all melodic lines.

V. Study the key relationships.

VI. Analyze the basic rhythmic structure of the entire work.

VII. Study the work's intellectual form and content.
VIII. Study the work's emotional content.

Below are listed several ways by which score study can be approached. There may be some controversy as to which is really the ideal way; they are given here simply as a guide.

1. Playing the score on the piano:

This takes some prowess on the piano, but with practice anyone can gain a degree of expertise. It is of course, much easier to play from a condensed score. At least this way the conductor will have a good idea of the harmonies and general flow of the melody.

2. Formal and informal analyzation:

This merely means looking over the score to see where the themes appear and re-appear; where there are changes in meter, key, tempo, style, etc.

3. Mistake-monitoring a la "musical E.S.P.":

This is a system by which the conductor looks through the music to see where he thinks his group will have trouble. He might mark these areas with a big "X" (in pencil that can be erased later) and comment on them before the first playing is to take place.

4. Singing the parts:

This is discussed in the booklet by Neilson and Holvik mentioned above.

5. Playing the parts on your instrument:

Most persons receiving a degree in music education have at least one instrument which they are quite expert in playing. Using this to play through the various band parts would give a good idea of the problems to be encountered and how the internal structure of the composition is put together.

6. Writing out a mapped progress:

This is merely listing on a sheet of paper *what* happens *when*. It is similar to number 2 above—a kind of analyzation but aimed more toward who plays what where. This might be likened to a cue-sheet.

7. Listening to a recording:

Some people may find this suggestion appalling, but more and more musicians are becoming aware that listening to a fine recording of a work helps them to think how they would render the same composition. It may be argued that this will lead them to the same interpretation as that of the conductor who did the recording. This may be true, but what is wrong with that? Especially if it is one of the many fine recordings by leading band conductors—in which case imitation might not be a bad idea at all!

8. Conducting a record:

There is a great temptation, when sitting in front of a stereo with a beautiful work unfolding before you and the score in hand, to wave your arms. Since this has a tendency (in the case of cues and changes of tempo) to teach you to follow the record, it is not too great a crime. Constant and repeated work through a score this way, however, gives you only a superficial look at what is going on. There is a tendency for you to learn the work by following and superficially memorizing the melody rather than by digging into the "meat" of the work and the initiative to "lead."

9. Learning it on the band:

This is what is done perhaps far too often. It is the thing one should guard against. The fact that the band is sight reading does not mean the conductor should be following suit. It is of course excellent practice when the band is sight reading works, for the band director to do the same. This should be done when the group is preparing to sight read at a contest. In this case, prior study on the director's part should be avoided.

It is readily known that the better the conductor knows the score himself, the sooner the band will learn it. The greatest asset in knowing the score thoroughly *before* the band gets it is that the conductor will have more time to help the band through the work rather than having to direct his entire efforts to finding his own way.

Rehearsal Hall Preparation

Only with proper planning can the rehearsal period be utilized efficiently. This means that all routine adjustments should be made before the period begins. Student help can be organized to arrange chairs, adjust electronic equipment to be used, hand out folders, and do the hundred and one things necessary to set the rehearsal in order. Much can be accomplished in a short time if the director has the preparation systematized. It is just as important to plan the preparation as it is to plan the actual rehearsal itself. Here is a suggested list of procedures to be repeated daily:

1. *Chairs:* Someone must be in charge of seeing that there are sufficient numbers of chairs and that they are spaced properly. It is advantageous to mark the rehearsal floor somehow so that the rows can be consistently placed in the same proximity.
2. *Music stands:* Another person should be in charge of seeing that there are sufficient music stands and that they are placed in front of the chairs where they will be needed.
3. *Music:* The music librarian or student with a study hall just before band rehearsal must pass out all music to be used. Music should never be passed out during a rehearsal. The only exception to this is when the band director decides to sight read a piece, but even here the music could be in specially designated envelopes.

4. *Order of rehearsal:* Much time can be saved during the course of the rehearsal if the music to be used is written on the front chalk board and the students are trained to place the compositions in the order shown.

5. *Percussion:* The percussion section leader or one of the section's members should arrange the percussion instruments before the period begins. He will be able to tell what instruments are to be used by the list of music placed on the chalk board.

6. *Special equipment:* Someone should be in charge of setting up and adjusting all special equipment like a phonograph, tape recorder, metronome, stroboscope, etc., before the period begins.

7. *Visitors:* Some arrangements should be made in case a visitor should come to the rehearsal. Simply placing a few chairs next to the door will suffice.

Warm-up and Tune-up: How to Start Out Right

The warm-up and tune-up segments are most often combined, i.e., there may be individual tuning via a stroboscope upon entering the rehearsal room, then a few warm-up exercises followed by general or specific tuning again. Also, at various intervals throughout the rehearsal there may be another few minutes spent on tuning or spot-checking certain individuals or sections. This retuning is especially necessary if the bandsmen come into a warm room from a wintery outdoors or enter an air-conditioned room on a very hot day.

If the band members have some organized form of technical instruction, i.e., private lessons, class lessons or technic classes, then the fourth item (technical drill) would be deleted from the rehearsal period.

This technical drill is also a combined item. It may simply be part of the warm-up period, ranging from a few minutes spent on playing various scales, scale patterns, rhythm and articulation exercises, to a completely organized and systematized curriculum for the bandsmen's technical development.

The determining factor as to the extent of time spent on this is the amount of work done by bandsmen outside the regular rehearsals and the organization of the total program. A band cannot become successful just by playing band music and more band music. It is an absolute necessity that the program constantly continue the development of the individual's instrumental technics—his facility to manipulate his instrument in all ways called for by the music the band desires to perform today and in the future. This technic, to be sure, is not developed solely so he can play band music but so individuals can successfully participate in other musical adventures as well.

Following these preliminaries the group would be ready for what is commonly called the "warm-up march." This is not to imply that a warm-up march should fit into this slot but that a march is not to be the very first thing on the rehearsal docket. A march is a very fast, wide-ranged type of composition that does not properly prepare a group mentally or physically for the rehearsal. A simpler piece with which the group is familiar, one that calls for fairly long phrases and that is well within convenient ranges of the instruments, would be best in this slot. This composition would act as a secondary warm-up period and one that contains more variety of color and ensemble-coordinating activity. If the band is working on something like a prelude and fugue for its next concert, this would be an excellent place for the rehearsal proper to start.

The band's ability to perfect concert numbers is significantly related to its ability to sight read. If a band has low sight-reading abilities it will have to figure each new piece out laboriously, section by section or even measure by measure. Bands of this type, as a result, will find it necessary to spend months preparing for one concert. Their rehearsals will be very boring to the conductor and the members alike. In circumstances like this, rehearsals become endless sessions of rote learning.

Because sight reading can be taught through an explained knowledge of music theory, some discussion of this area is necessary. To do this during a rehearsal, however, is an unwise use of that time if other opportunities are available—i.e., if the band program includes sectional rehearsals and/or technic classes.

Playing a familiar piece at the end of the rehearsal is for purely psychological purposes. This is especially necessary if some very hard work has been done on new compositions, as it allows the band members to leave the rehearsal with a "good taste" in their mouths. It acts as a little dessert at the end of the musical meal.

The piece used could be a rousing march, a piece done on the last concert that went well and that may be used in the future. It may simply be a piece played in the past that the band enjoys. Selections from Broadway shows fit well into a situation like this —if they are well known to the students.

If the band has an active student staff they could be allowed to set up their favorite tune for the day. They would meet periodically to make a list of those songs they like to play. The conductor should oversee the selection to be certain its range is appropriate. Embouchures will no doubt be tired by this time and should not be additionally taxed with excessively high or loud playing. If the piece should, as most of them often do, end very loudly, keep the rehearsal under control even at this late hour by insisting on not a *fff* at the end but an *ff* or better yet an *f*. Allowing undisciplined blowing at the end of the rehearsal defeats the purpose one has been trying to establish.

In this segment of the rehearsal the bandsmen must come to understand that "having fun" does not necessarily mean that all discipline (controlled playing) is thrown out the window.

The ninth item on the list can be interspersed throughout the rehearsal; it does not necessarily come last. Announcements are actually useful in several ways. They not only impart information but if used wisely can also aid in maintaining discipline throughout the rehearsal and give the band time to rest their embouchures.

Announcements can best be placed in the rehearsal somewhere in the middle and at the end, depending upon the length of rehearsal. General announcements may be advantageously given at some point during the rehearsal proper. As this is the most concentrated section, a slight pause would be good either at the midpoint or about three-quarters of the way through.

The announcements given at this time must not be the sort that would result in any form of discussion between band members or between the director and band members. They should be purely informative. Controversial items must be saved for the end of the rehearsal. An item that might raise a need for discussion coming at the midpoint invariably will disrupt the rest of the rehearsal, not only because it would be time consuming but also because it could be of a nature that would divide the band into opinion camps. This is not to imply that differences of opinion must not be tolerated but merely that they should not arise at a time when unity is of greatest necessity. Save the controversial subjects for the end of the rehearsal.

Announcements that are directly involved with the offices of someone on the student staff, such as the student business manager, the student librarian, etc., should be made by the respective student. It is very easy for the band director to make all announcements, but having the officers give their own announcements gives them some leadership responsibilities and teaches the band that they can look to these individuals for information they may need. This in turn encourages more responsibility on the part of the individual officers. Also this gives them some experience in talking in front of a large group.

Preparational Procedures

The purpose of the following discussion of concert program preparation is to emphasize the need for a varied and wide use of all methods of rehearsing, and to give a perspective of the entire problem. The wise band director will vary his procedure from day to day by using a combination of the following methods while stressing the plan best adapted to his immediate needs.

All program numbers need a beginning-to-end reading the first time they are presented to the band in order that the pupils may obtain a bird's eye view of the selection. Then after careful analysis and much individual and sectional drill the numbers can be solidified by another beginning-to-end-reading.

When to Use the Beginning-to-End Method

Before any intensive drill on a composition can begin, it is a good idea to give the band members an overall view of the composition. This is done simply by reading through from beginning to end, with stops only to get everyone together. The stops can be made to point out the type of interpretation that should be activated at a particular point, or very general things like the fact that the tempo is lagging or the overall dynamic level is too loud, etc.

Many directors make the mistake of considering this a method that should always be used in perfecting a composition. They think that by playing a composition over and over from beginning to end, the band members will finally learn it. Quite the contrary is true, however. Constantly using this method can result in students' responding to sounds they hear around them. It can result in their learning the composition wrong. This most often happens with rhythmic figures. After the students have played through a composition many, many times, the incorrect figures can become so ingrained that it is almost impossible to correct them at some later date.

This approach should be used only if the composition is somewhat within the band's reading ability. A composition that is extremely difficult should not be approached in this manner. Under normal conditions a difficult number should be approached by the section-spotting method.

After a composition has been worked on for a number of weeks or is well within the band's reading ability, the beginning-to-end method might be used most of the time. This gives the group an overall picture of the work as it proceeds. This is the method to use for compositions just prior to a performance when the internal sections have been worked out and most all the parts can be played with some facility.

The Error Barrier Technique

This is similar to the beginning-to-end method, except that rarely will the band reach the end of the composition in any one rehearsal. In this procedure the band starts at the beginning but each time an error occurs the group is stopped. That error is immediately worked out. When it can be performed with accuracy the playing continues.

Section Spotting

This is similar to the error barrier method except that the director brings to the rehearsal a list of those areas or sections in which the band has had trouble or in which he anticipates trouble will occur. Normally this would be used only after the band has played a composition several times. It would also be used if there are only a very few rehearsals between the inception of the rehearsing of the materials and the concert. This is the type of rehearsing a community band would follow when they have only one rehearsal and a concert each week. This method must not be used constantly with school bands because it is very frustrating to the musicians to play only small bits and snatches of a work. However, this is probably the most fruitful method for it spots difficulties and works over them until some degree of perfection is reached. Bands who do not use this system at times probably never really perfect an entire composition, for there are always those few measures that are extremely difficult technically, rhythmically, dynamically, intonation-wise, or whatever.

Error Marking

This can be very effective with a band if its members are accustomed to taking their music home to practice. The band uses the beginning-to-end method, but each time a problem arises the director stops and has the problem areas circled in pencil by the members of sections in which the problem occurred. In this way the students could immediately attack the problem areas in any composition.

The Talk-through Method

This method is the one used and allowed at sight-reading contests. Here the director points out to this players the spots in the composition that may cause trouble—such places as changes of key, changes of meter, drastic or excessive changes in dynamics, long diminuendos, important accents, strange or unusual rhythms, etc. The director may sing through a particularly difficult section or even clap a rhythm that might be confusing.

This system is also of great value after the band has played a composition several times. The director can mention troublesome areas in the composition, particularly if previously a change of key has been missed, a dynamic change has gone unnoticed, etc.

Effective Use of the Baton in Rehearsals

Much time is wasted in rehearsals if the conductor does not (or perhaps cannot) use the baton. There should be no necessity to "tell" the band to play soft, or loud, or *crescendo,* or *diminuendo,* or *accelerando,* or *ritard.* These things and hundreds more should be done with the baton, not with the mouth. Two ideas that can help in improving one's ability to show these are a mirror and a system called psychological conducting (Psychological conducting is discussed thoroughly in *The Modern Conductor* by Elizabeth A. H. Green, published by Prentice-Hall, Inc.)

Practicing the score in front of a mirror while singing the main themes will give a picture of what is being shown to the band. If a change occurs and it is not shown by the baton or some other conducting device, how can a band be expected to make the change? Isn't the band supposed to be following the conductor? Shouldn't it be assumed that the band can read what is on the score and follow those directions? Not so! Besides, if the conductor does not show any change, should he expect his band to show them anyway?

Max Rudolf in his book *The Conductor's Art* makes the following observations on when to stop and use the voice for directions and under what circumstances:

1. Before interrupting, be sure of what you are going to say.
2. Educate your [band] so that everyone stops right at your signal and then observes silence.
3. Begin your comments without hesitation, and whenever possible formulate them in terms of clearly defined technical advice.
4. Never say "once more" after interrupting without giving a good reason, unless things have gone wrong to such an extent that the necessity for repeating is obvious.

5. Frequently remarks are addressed not to all musicians but to sections or individual players. In this case, first identify the instruments concerned, then the passage in question, then explain why you are not satisfied. Discussions of extended solo passages ought to take place in private, which is preferable to lengthy explanations in the presence of the [band].
6. Do not discuss musical details without being sure that the players have turned to the right page and know exactly what you are talking about.
7. Once you have begun working on a passage you must persist until improvement is noticeable, unless a player is not capable of coping with a particular problem because of technical limitations.
8. Announce distinctly the place where the music is to be resumed. "We begin three bars before letter 'X' " cannot be misunderstood, but it is safer to say "the third bar after letter 'Y'." To find the place some players may have to count many measures of rest, so allow sufficient time and perhaps repeat the announcement. Materials should be marked abundantly with rehearsal numbers and letters.

   (If there are a number of measures between each rehearsal letter, train the band to count with the conductor by saying: "Count with me starting at letter D, that's one, now—2, 3, 4, 5, 6," etc. After announcing the procedure, look to see that each bandsman has his finger on the place where the counting is to start—letter D.)

9. After proper announcement, resume the music as soon as practicable, and without lingering.
10. Spoken comments while the musicians are playing should be used sparingly by the conductor.[1]

---

[1] From *The Conductor's Art* edited by Carl Bamberger. Copyright © 1965 by McGraw-Hill, Inc., pp. 281–282. Used with permission of McGraw-Hill Book Co.

Achieving Rehearsal Objectives

In a clinic outline distributed by the H. & A. Selmer Company, Nilo Hovey set down ten objectives for band rehearsals. Mr. Hovey states: "Every rehearsal should contribute to the improvement of one or more of the following elements of effective ensemble performance:

    (1) Intonation
    (2) Tone quality
    (3) Rhythmic accuracy
    (4) Precision of attacks and uniformity of release
    (5) Clarity of articulation
    (6) Control of tempo
    (7) Technical facility
    (8) Control of total dynamic level
    (9) Proper emphasis of thematic material
 (10) Interpretation—phrasing and style." [2]

When rehearsing the band the director should use the above as a mental check-list and work over the band much as a watch repairman works over a watch that is not functioning properly. Just as the repairman studies the workings of a watch to see what needs to be done to achieve a perfect function in keeping with "father time," so too the band director studies his score to see how the band must function to achieve the composer's intent.

Through his careful observances of the interactions of the various parts of a watch the repairman can then dissect the instrument and correct those parts that are in error. When someone takes his watch in to a repairman he first describes the problem: It does not keep time. It runs too fast. It runs too slow. It does not run at all, or the wind stem is broken off. The band director upon taking up a score immediately seeks to find out what it is

---

[2] Nilo Hovey, "Efficient Rehearsal Procedures for the Concert Band—A Clinic Outline" (Elkhart, Indiana: H. & A. Selmer, Inc.).

all about—it is a march, a Baroque transcription of an organ fugue, an original contemporary work with a Romantic style or a Contemporary tone poem. All these things will determine which cogs in the band's technics will probably need attention.

Using Musical E.S.P.

When one takes his watch to the repairman and says that it simply does not work, several items rush through the repairman's head, zeroing in on what is probably wrong. This happens even before he has taken the back off the watch. The outward appearance of the watch itself gives him many clues. A lot of dust accumulated on the face of the watch, or several tool marks along the edges where the watch comes together, may give the repairman an idea that something serious might be wrong. In a similar manner the band director, even before he gives the first downbeat, can anticipate several things that will be wrong with the rendition of a particular composition. Looking over his small trombone section, for example, he will zero in on a balance problem when counter-melodies occur. A large trumpet section will immediately indicate that the melodic line in the clarinet section will probably be lost when both have the line together— especially if there are eight trumpets and maybe only ten or twelve clarinets. A large tuba section may indicate a ponderous rendition of a scherzo movement.

What to Look For

The items that may be wrong will, of course, depend upon the ability of the band as a whole, the ability of individuals within the various sections and the character and/or size of the various sections. A high school band will obviously make different types and kinds of mistakes with varying degrees of error than will a junior high or college band. However, certain elements of performance or more accurately, certain problematic elements of performance are common to all types of large ensembles and need careful attention.

The problems will first be merely stated and then in later chapters will be shown: (1) what is needed or what can be done that may result in the problems being straightened out; (2) activities that can be carried on that will improve the rendition of the particular technic; and (3) ramifications of stylistic considerations and how the various technics must thus be handled or manipulated.

Many of the problems that are encountered in a band's performance cannot be corrected as a direct result of the rehearsing processes. Many technics or the proper rendering of the technics needed can only be accomplished by individual skill. It has been said, and rightly so, that playing band music—and more band music—and more band music will not necessarily make for a better band. For this reason the band's program must include some kind of individual instruction and a program that encourages individual practice.

The following is a complete list of problem areas. The list is not meant to be held in the band director's hand and checked off item by item as the music progresses, but is given as a reminder of the things that can and do go wrong with the band's performance. It is meant as an antidote to: "Gee, it sure doesn't sound right, but I can't figure out for the life of me what is wrong." It should also prevent the rehearsal "disease" of saying: "Let's play it once more," without specific directives of why it is being done again.

Perhaps the list could be used as an in-depth diagnostic checklist while listening to a tape recording of a composition the band has been working on in rehearsal. Since the list is so extensive, the composition could be listened to several times, with those items on the list under tone and intonation noted on the first playing, two other items noted on a second playing, and possibly the remainder on a third and/or fourth playing.

Checklist of Key Problem Areas

TONE

1. Is the band's tone resonant (live and buoyant—not "dead")?
2. Does the tone have compactness (does it not have a tendency to "spread")?
3. Does the band's tone reflect the character(s) of the composition?
4. Does the tone change when the character of the composition changes?
5. Is the tone too bright for the composition?
6. Is the tone too dark for the composition?
7. Is the tone brilliant enough at appropriate spots?
8. Is the tone resonant enough at appropriate spots?
9. Does the band have sufficient sonority (richness produced by "bottom to top" sound)?
10. Is there sufficient sonority in the upper parts?
11. Is there sufficient sonority in the middle parts?
12. Is there sufficient sonority in the lower parts?
13. Is the tone of the upper parts resonant (not strident)?
14. Is the tone of the middle parts resonant (not dull)?
15. Is the tone of the lower parts resonant and clean (not tubby and muddy)?
16. Does the bass drum add unwanted "rumble" to the total sound?
17. Is the tone consistent at various dynamic levels?
18. Does the tone spread when playing loud?
19. Does the tone quality suffer when playing loud?
20. Does the tone become strident when playing loud?
21. Does the tone quality suffer when playing soft?
22. Does the tone quality decay when playing soft?
23. Does the tone become dull when playing soft?
24. Does the tone suffer when various sections (which sections?) play in the lower register?
25. Does the tone suffer when various sections (which sections?) play in the middle register?
26. Does the tone suffer when various sections (which sections?) play in the upper register?

27. Does the tone suffer when playing rapid passages?
28. Does the tone suffer when playing staccato passages?
29. Does control of the tone suffer when playing sustained passages?
30. Are there any unnecessary mechanical noises (particularly in very soft passages)?

INTONATION

1. How is the general intonation?
2. Does the band play generally flat?
3. Does the band play generally sharp?
4. Is there faulty intonation between sections?
5. Is there faulty intonation within the woodwind section?
6. Is there faulty intonation within the flute section?
7. Is there faulty intonation within the double reed section?
8. Is there faulty intonation within the clarinet section?
9. Is there faulty intonation within the saxophone section?
10. Is there faulty intonation within the brass section?
11. Is there faulty intonation within the cornet section?
12. Is there faulty intonation within the trumpet section?
13. Is there faulty intonation within the French horn section?
14. Is there faulty intonation within the trombone section?
15. Is there faulty intonation within the baritone section?
16. Is there faulty intonation within the tuba section?
17. Is there faulty intonation between the timpani and the band?
18. Is there faulty intonation within the solo and accompaniment?
19. Is there faulty intonation within the soli instruments?
20. Are those playing the solo line in tune?
21. Are those playing accompaniment lines in tune?
22. Are those playing the counter-melody in tune?
23. Is there faulty intonation within the chordal structure?
24. Is there faulty intonation in octave combinations?
25. Is intonation affected by dynamic changes?

BALANCE

1. Is the melodic line too soft/loud?
2. Is the supporting harmonic line too soft/loud?
3. Is the counter-melody too soft/loud?
4. Is the accompaniment too soft/loud?

5. Are the voices within the accompaniment properly balanced?
6. Are chords evenly balanced?
7. Is the root of the chord(s) too soft/loud?
8. Is the third of the chord(s) too soft/loud?
9. Is the fifth of the chord(s) too soft/loud?
10. Is the dissonant interval(s) too soft/loud?
11. Is the woodwind section too soft/loud?
12. Is the brass section too soft/loud?
13. Is the percussion section too soft/loud?
14. Is the flute section too soft/loud?
15. Is the oboe section too soft/loud?
16. Is the clarinet section too soft/loud?
17. Is the first flute too soft/loud?
18. Is the second flute too soft/loud?
19. Is the first oboe too soft/loud?

BLEND

1. Does the organization sound like a total unit (i.e., no single section or groups of instruments standing out in tutti passages)?
2. Is there a blending of sounds within the flute section?
3. Is there a blending of sounds within the oboe section?
4. Is there a blending of sounds within the bassoon section?
5. Is there a blending of sounds within the clarinet section?
6. Is there a blending of sounds within the low clarinets?
7. Is there a blending of sounds within the saxophone section?
8. Is there a blending of sounds within the cornet/trumpet section?
9. Is there a blending of sounds within the French horn section?
10. Is there a blending of sounds within the trombone section?
11. Is there a blending of sounds within the baritone section?
12. Is there a blending of sounds within the tuba section?
13. Is there a blending of sounds within the percussion section?
14. Does the flute section blend with the rest of the band?
15. Does the oboe section blend with the rest of the band?
16. Does the bassoon section blend with the rest of the band?
17. Does the clarinet section blend with the rest of the band?
19. Does the saxophone section blend with the rest of the band?
20. Does the cornet section blend with the best of the band?
21. Does the trumpet section blend with the rest of the band?

22. Does the French horn section blend with the rest of the band?
23. Does the trombone section blend with the rest of the band?
24. Does the baritone section blend with the rest of the band?
25. Does the tuba section blend with the rest of the band?
26. Does the percussion section blend with the rest of the band?
27. Does the triangle sound blend with the rest of the band?
28. Do the cymbals (where appropriate) blend with the rest of the band?

PRECISION

1. Is the ensemble clean sounding (i.e., not muddy)?
2. Are attacks clean and precise?
3. Are releases clean and precise?
4. Are notes placed in their proper rhythmic position?
5. Is the length of the note(s) too short?
6. Are similar notes within a passage of uniform length and quality?
7. Are accents clean?
8. Are accents well defined?
9. Are afterbeats clean and precise?
10. Is there precision within the ensemble (not ragged)?
11. Are fermatas released accurately and uniformly?
12. Is the ensemble steady on rhythmic changes?
13. Does the bass drum follow the baton?
14. Are staccato notes played with the same length throughout the band?
15. When an anacrusis appears, is it clearly articulated?
16. Do solo passages have clear and clean articulation?

RHYTHM

1. Are whole notes held for their full value?
2. Are dotted-half notes held for their full duration?
3. Are half notes held for their full duration?
4. Are quarter notes that appear at the ends of phrases given full value?
5. Is the eighth in a dotted-quarter and eighth note figure given its proper value?
6. Are dotted-eighth and sixteenth note figures played proportionally correctly?

7. Are consecutive eighth notes played evenly?
8. Are triplets evenly spaced (not played like two sixteenths and an eighth)?
9. Are running eighths or sixteenths evenly played (not rushed)?
10. Is the note after an anacrusis anticipated?

STYLE

1. Is the style of the composition broad enough?
2. Are the choral-type passages fully sustained?
3. Do phrase endings need more blocking?
4. Are phrase endings too abrupt?
5. Is there a need for more detachment of the notes?
6. Is there a need for a more marcato style?
7. Is there a correct interpretation of the rhythmic dot?
8. Is there a correct interpretation of the staccato dot?
9. Are dissonances treated properly?
10. Are appoggiaturas played correctly?
11. Are trills played correctly?
12. Is the vibrato used properly?
13. Is the mordent played correctly?
14. Is the gruppetto played correctly?
15. Is the style too heavy?
16. Is there a need for more lyricism?
17. Is there a need for more sostenuto?
18. Is there a need for more espressivo playing?
19. Is there too much espressivo playing?
20. Is there a need for more rubato?
21. Is there a need for less rubato?
22. Is there a need for more rhythmic energy?
23. Is there a need for less vigor?

TEMPO

1. Is the tempo too fast?
2. Is the tempo too slow?
3. Does the tempo slow down?
4. Does the tempo seem to drag?
5. Does the tempo speed up?
6. Is the tempo too fast for some players?
7. Is the tempo too fast for the band?

8. Does the tempo have a rhythmic drive (if called for)?
9. Does the tempo seem to be rushed?
10. In slow passages does the tempo tend to slow down?
11. When there is a slow rhythmic flow does the tempo tend to slow down?
12. During soft passages does the tempo tend to slow down?
13. Does the tempo seem to speed up?
14. When rapid notes are encountered, does the tempo seem to speed up?
15. Does the tempo seem to speed up in loud passages?
16. Is there too much contrast at tempo changes?
17. Is the tempo change well defined?
18. Is the tempo change clean?
19. Does the tempo change occur at the instant called for?

PHRASING

1. Are phrase endings cut too short?
2. Do phrases sound all alike?
3. Are phrases clearly defined?
4. Do the phrases flow and lead to the climax?
5. Does the dynamic intensity ebb and flow with the rise and fall of the phrase?

INTERPRETATION

1. Does the melody line contain proper amounts of shading?
2. Is there enough separation of accented notes?
3. Is there sufficient distinction between legato and staccato?
4. Are staccato notes played smoothly (not rough)?
5. Are staccato notes played too short?
6. Are breaths taken in the proper places?
7. Is there too much time taken for the breath?
8. Is the tempo too fast?
9. Is the tempo too slow?
10. Are *rit., rall., accel., cresc., decresc., dim.,* etc., too abrupt?
11. Are *rit., rall., accel., cresc., decresc., dim.,* etc., executed clearly (can they be heard or are they too subtle)?
12. Is the performance mechanical?
13. Does the performance catch the mood, character or spirit of the composition?

DYNAMICS

1. Are the dynamic variations in keeping with the mood, spirit and/or character of the composition?
2. Are the dynamic levels active (not an anemic mezzo-forte or constant fortissimo)?
3. Are there graduations within a single dynamic panel?
4. Is the crescendo within the mood, spirit and/or character of the phrase?
5. Is the diminuendo within the mood, spirit and/or character of the phrase?
6. Is the gradual dynamic change gradual?
7. Are sudden dynamic changes sudden?
8. Is the crescendo as obvious as it should be?
9. Is the crescendo too sudden (reaches the climax too soon)?
10. Does the crescendo start too loud?
11. Does the crescendo end too loud?
12. Does the height of the crescendo coincide with the height of the phrase or melody?
13. Is the diminuendo as obvious as it should be?
14. Is the diminuendo as subtle as it should be?
15. Is the diminuendo too sudden?
16. Does the low point in the phrase or melody coincide with the low point in the dynamic level?
17. Does the diminuendo start too softly?
18. Does the diminuendo end too softly?
19. Are there subtle differences between *mf* and *f*?
20. Are there subtle differences between *mp* and *p*?
21. Are piano passages too loud?
22. Are piano passages too soft?
23. Are forte passages too loud?
24. Are forte passages too soft?
25. Are fortissimo passages too loud?
26. Are fortissimo passages too soft?
27. Are accents in keeping with the mood, spirit and/or character of the section?
28. Are accents in keeping with the prevailing dynamic level?
29. Are dynamic changes anticipated?
30. Are dynamic changes started too late?

four

Creating a Better Sound Through Proper Warm-up/Tune-up

Approaches for the Initial Tuning

There are three basic methods by which the initial tuning can be accomplished: group self-tuning (the most often used), individual self-tuning, or conductor-directed tuning.

The group self-tuning is the type that takes the least amount of time. For this, one member of the band or an electronic device gives the pitch and each member of the band, en masse, individually tunes his instrument. This method of tuning, although the most frequently used, is perhaps the least successful except in the most mature groups.

If a band member is to tune his instrument by a given standard he must be able to hear that standard and compare his pitch to that standard. However, when everyone in the band plays immediately after the standard is given, it is practically impossible for anyone to hear his own pitch. It does help if the player puts his finger up and closes off his ear. Ideally, each person in the band, after hearing the pitch, will play one rather short note very softly so his neighbor can hear his own pitch. Too often, this moment of free tuning turns into a fiasco of scale, arpeggio and melody study at the *fortissimo* level.

This group self-tuning might be done a little more conscientiously if the band members were taught a routine and not allowed to deviate from it. The procedure could go something like this:

1. The tuning note is sounded.
2. Each student then individually plays his tuning note two or three times *piano*. To be effective this note and only this note must be played—and played *piano*.
3. The director calls a halt to the playing after about five seconds. It does not take any more than five seconds to play the turning note once and make the necessary adjustments.
4. The tuning note is sounded a second time for a double check.
5. Again, the band would be allowed to play the tuning note on their instruments.
6. A third check could be made, at which time the director would allow another five seconds of playing for a final check.

A technic that sometimes can be used in conjunction with the group self-tuning is to have the band as a whole hum the pitch before playing. This gives them a very personal standard to match with their instrument. They hear the pitch mentally as well as orally before playing.

The tuning-up period can lead to a general breakdown in discipline. Coming at the beginning of the rehearsal it can be disastrous as it may very well set the attitude for the rest of the rehearsal. Letting the students blow *fortissimo* or play scales and runs up and down is not only a great disadvantage to them but also makes it difficult if not impossible for the more conscientious players to tune carefully. Time and time again this group self-tuning becomes merely a battle to see who can blow the loudest or get in the most runs during those few minutes of released time.

An adjunct to the group self-tuning would be a sectional self-tuning. The tuning note would be given, after which the conductor would designate one section to tune themselves. After this section is tuned, the tuning note would be given again and another section allowed to tune. The most logical procedure would be to start with the flute section, then the double reeds, the clarinets, etc., down through the score, leaving the tubas till last. They too often are the forgotten few way in the back. Do not always go in score order but skip around. The tubas would indeed be pleased if they were chosen first.

This tuning by sections alleviates some of the loud competitive blowing.

Giving the Pitch

The traditional method of giving a single pitch by which all the instruments tune themselves is through the use of the oboe. This method comes down to us through the orchestra but in most cases is far too inadequate for the present context of the school band.

An accomplished oboe player can play as much as one-half step flat by manipulating his embouchure and almost a quarter-step sharp. In the case of the young oboist his pitch may vary this much without his even being aware of it. In the hands of a young oboist—and of many who have been playing for a number of years—the pitch is exceedingly unstable and not at all adequate for purposes of tuning the band.

Many band directors select one of their better players to sound the first pitch no matter what instrument he might be playing. If the band contains a very fine oboist, by all means use him. It would be best to select a treble instrument—one that would sound in the range of the band's overall range. For this purpose a cornet or clarinet would perhaps be the most felicitous. Selecting the first clarinetist would be advantageous because he is out in front of the group and can easily stand up and face the band when sounding the tuning note. Unless the first flutist has an exceptionally good, rich tone, its quality would not be sufficiently strong for the purpose. The cornet would make an excellent pitch-standard giver.

Electronic devices, especially the portable ones, make excellent standards for establishing the pitch—certainly a lot better than a young oboist. Though the strobotuner is an excellent device for individual work, a device that emits a tone is far better for tuning the band as a whole. The value of the tuning bar is great, but it is far overshadowed by such devices as the Tempo-Tuner (Selmer) or the Peterson Chromatic Tuner (Electro-Musical Products of Worth, Illinois). Whereas the tuning bar's tone lasts only a few seconds, the electronically produced tone of the tuners emits a sustained pitch. If neither of these devices is available a band director should consider making use of such things as a set of orchestra bells or the chimes. The chimes are excellent because their tone is sustained long enough for the band to perceive the pitch and is also loud enough to be adequately heard by everyone.

Which Pitch?

Ralph R. Pottle in his book, *Tuning the School Band and Orchestra,* states: "It is regrettable that tradition has decreed tuning the B-Flat clarinet to its C or B—sounding Bb$_4$ or A$_4$—which are two of its least sensitive tones to barrel adjustment. The proper amount of pull is best determined by sounding and adjusting to the sensitive throat tones . . . . but the player should also check other notes before completing the process of tuning." [1]

Dr. Pottle goes on to explain that though first space F is best for the tuning of the clarinet it is not the best note for all other instruments in the band. The appendix to Dr. Pottle's book,

---

[1] Ralph R. Pottle, *Tuning the School Band and Orchestra* (Hammond, Louisiana: Ralph R. Pottle, 1970), p. 20.

written by Mark Hindsley, contains a set of "Tuning Guides" showing the best notes for each instrument. These tuning guides are published separately and are designed for placing in band folios for individual reference.

Rather than sounding one note it is best to give several so that each instrument may tune to its most appropriate pitch. Thus an E-flat would be sounded for the clarinets, a B-flat for the flutes, oboes, trumpets, trombones and tubas, a C for the alto saxophone and an F for the bassoon and French horn.

If only one note can be given, i.e., during the course of a concert, then perhaps the best tone for the entire band would be a concert F. This would allow for a good check for the clarinet barrel location and gives an open pitch that the brasses can match.

Four Steps in the Warm-up Period

Though the term "warm-up" has become an accepted part of the musicians' jargon it is actually a misnomer and somewhat ambiguous. What is generally meant by this term is, in part, to gently stimulate the lip muscles in preparation for continued playing.

There are actually four processes that should be a part of the warm-up. The first is this gentle stimulation of the lip muscles. Also to be considered in certain cases is a re-stimulation of the muscles that provide for finger and tongue dexterity. This is also a time for warming up the instrument. This warming-up is very slight to be sure but is a necessary process for continuing good intonation throughout the rehearsal or concert. Additionally this initial period of starting the band rehearsal is a time for toning up (musically) the bandsmen's brains or minds or attitudes and for toning up the ears. The initial tuning process is of little value if the students are not provided with the stimulus to listen carefully. Perhaps this states it more clearly: preparing them psychologically to listen and to discipline themselves for the concentrated work that will ensue; or—more simply: getting them settled down and in the mood.

The gentle stimulation of the lip muscles must be just that—*gentle*. This is done by playing for several minutes (some writers on the subject suggest five or even ten minutes) in the lower register of the instrument. This generally means keeping the cornets on the staff, starting with their written middle C. The traditional B-flat warm-up scale is an excellent point at which to start. This is, however, only the starting point and it does have some drawbacks which will be discussed.

Besides keeping the instrument within an easy range it is also most advantageous that the band play softly and in a sustained fashion. The B-flat scale played with eight counts on each scale step at MM-96 works well in this conjunction. Besides providing a simple stimulation of the lip, these long tones will allow bands-men to listen for various other aspects of technic like intonation, blend, balance and tone quality.

The director must not automatically assume that the bandsmen will keep these various ideas in mind while playing. He must constantly call attention to these facets and enforce listening. A danger in the constant use of the B-flat warm-up scale is that band members may fall into a musical robot attitude. Even if they do, however, this session is not a total failure as their lips will automatically warm up even if their minds are on next week's picnic or last period's history exam. The director must constantly seek ways of varying the warm-up routine so that it is constantly an educational experience. There will be, further in this chapter, some ideas for doing this.

The term "warm-up" is also applied to the instruments—i.e., warming up the instrument. Here too, the term should not be taken too literally. It is merely used to find out at which pitch the instrument is sounding in relation to the temperature of the room.

After finding out at which pitch it is sounding, the instrument must then be altered so that it achieves the standard being used.

The air on the inside of the instrument, when it is being played, is about 90° F. because the player's breath is 98.6° F. If the temperature of the room is 70° F. the temperature in the instrument would be about 90° at the mouthpiece and 70° at the bell. The smaller instruments are more highly warmed by the breath than the larger ones.

It must not be assumed that just because the instrument was warmed up and tuned the pitch will remain constant. The instant the player ceases to play upon the instrument, the temperature at the mouthpiece begins to lower. A four-measure rest can change the temperature of the instrument considerably. Likewise, as the rehearsal or concert progresses the temperature of the room will rise. Not only will the mouthpiece end of the instrument remain warm longer but the bell end of the instrument will also be more warmed by the outside temperature.

Thus it would seem that it is impossible to play an instrument in tune, especially in consort with other instruments, considering that every time one has a rest (or an entire section has a rest) the instruments immediately begin cooling—and cooling at different rates. True, it is well-nigh impossible for a band to play in tune— except for one instrument we have at our command that, if educated and used properly, can make the difference—*the ear*. It is therefore perhaps more important to warm up the players' ears and minds than it is to warm up their instruments. By "warm up" in this context we mean to educate or re-educate or re-awaken the players' ears as they enter the rehearsal room, and alert their minds to the minute changes that occur in the pitch from a cold instrument in a cool room to a warm instrument to a highly warmed instrument in a highly warmed room.

An interesting light has been shed on this business of physically warming up the instrument by the Acoustical Society of America. Some research has found that changing temperatures do not have any great effect on the actual pitch inherent in the instrument. It has been found that a difference of as much as 28° is so minute that most ears cannot detect the difference.

More often than not it is the attitude of the director that determines whether the band warms up their ears through that vehicle called the brain. Simply allowing the bandsmen to play through the B-flat warm-up scale will not succeed in waking up their ears and minds to the tasks at hand. This can most easily be done by the director's carefully listening himself and calling attention to discrepancies that crop up. The director should assume a mental attitude of listening carefully. A play-acting attitude can help, provided it is not overdone: perhaps a furrowed brow, a tilted head, or a turning of the head so one ear is directed toward the erring section. Also, if a certain scale pitch is especially out of tune, do not just beat eight; hold it until the band corrects it, then with a nod of the head continue to the next pitch level.

How to Insure Careful Listening

One thing that can be done to encourage the bandsmen into an attitude of careful listening is to make them play their initial warm-up scale *piano*. This level must be rigidly enforced. They must not be allowed to play at a *forte* level or a *mezzo-forte* level, but *piano*—not even *mezzo-piano* but a real *piano*!

It may take some doing to get them down to the proper level, especially if they have been accustomed to blowing loudly in an undisciplined fashion upon entering the rehearsal room. The entire tenor of the rehearsal is often set by the manner in which this warm-up routine is started. If it is *very* carefully controlled, a warm-up using all the players' facilities for listening and thinking to play in a highly disciplined fashion, achieving the levels called for by the director, great psychological attitudes can be achieved. Playing the warm-up in a lackadaisical attitude may well mean the rest of the rehearsal will be the same—lackadaisical.

A Re-tuning

Following a short warm-up routine the standard pitch should be given again so the players can re-check their instruments.

Depending upon the time available, further care can be taken to insure that all sections are in tune. The following suggestions are given here not only as a means of tuning the group internally but also to act as ear warming-up exercises.

Proven Tuning Routines

Have the entire flute section, for example, play the tuning pitch. On the conductor's signal, all stop playing except one. If this one is not in tune with the rest it will be quite obvious. If the section is very large, like the clarinets, before they start playing the tuning note tell the group that upon the signal everyone is to stop playing except the first chair second and the fourth chair third, or some other such combination. Do not always call upon the first chair players of the various sections. They more often than not need it less than the back chair players. Have the tuning note played, then have the whole group play together. Upon the signal everyone will be able to see if the two left are in tune not only with each other but with the group as a whole. This technic need not be used only within one section. Six players from the horn section could be matched with six flutes or six clarinets, etc. For purposes of identifying this the procedure would be called "tutti to solo/soli tuning."

A type of add-on procedure can be used along these same lines. Have one person in a section play the tuning note. Now add a second person in that section. When this second person comes in, however, he must not be heard. He must blend in perfectly with the first player. This blending must not only be by pitch but by dynamics and tone quality also. The first person should play at least a good *mezzo-forte*. Once these two are "in phase" add a third, then a fourth, etc. All persons from the first to the last must keep playing the tone. They may drop out to take a breath but must come back in without being heard. In large sections it becomes difficult indeed to achieve any kind of perfection after four or five players have been added. So as not always to leave out the last few chair players—who need this training as much, if not more than any others—start in the middle of the section, or take the first chair, then the third, then the fifth, or take all the even-numbered players. Because they will be sitting some distance apart there is an added difficulty but try the first chair, then the last chair, then the second chair, then the second from the end, etc. One might also start from the middle and work out in both directions.

This technic can also be used effectively with different kinds of instruments. In this case, however, the timbre will be changed upon the addition of a different instrument, but the dynamics and the pitch must not be changed. Even though they are different instruments they should produce not two different and distinct tones but a combined timbre. This combined timbre should actually create a different sound. When an artist combines red and yellow he does not produce a red-yellow but an entirely new color. So too, bandsmen must achieve the creation of a new tone color. Through this procedure bandsmen can also come to understand some problems in balance. A trumpet playing *mezzo-forte* against a flute playing *mezzo-forte* does not achieve a balanced timbre, especially if the flute is in its lower range. The bandsmen must come to understand the differences in their colleagues' instruments, and must learn to compensate.

John Conlee suggests a routine he called "competitive tuning":
"After the band has warmed up, all members except percussion

stand. One member of the percussion section is appointed time-keeper and the tuning routine is timed each day, from the first note sounded to the last. Students play their tuning notes in a set order, from left to right across the first row, right to left across the second, left to right across the third, etc.

"As each note is sounded, the director pronounces it 'flat,' 'sharp,' or 'O.K.' If the note is 'O.K.' the student sits. If not, he remains standing for the next round. When the last person in the last row has sounded his note the procedure is repeated with those who remain standing, playing again and again until everyone is seated.

"The director may prefer to substitute 'yes' or 'no' for his readings, with the student deciding whether they are flat or sharp and being seated on 'yes.'

"How is this tuning 'competitive'? In several ways. First, the average student prefers to be seated as soon as possible. As the tuning progresses and the student remains standing, he is competing with his fellow students for the 'O.K.' that will allow him to sit. No student wants to be the last one standing.

"In addition to the competition between individual students the entire band is competing against time. A daily record is kept of the time taken for tuning. Each day we try to break this record. The daily time record increases student interest and at the same time speeds up the tuning process. There is little 'dead' time until all but one person is seated; then we must wait for his adjustments. These pauses, which add to the time total for the whole band, increase the discomfort of the person who is tuning and encourage him to make an effort to be seated more quickly the next time."

Mr. Conlee states that most bands can be tuned in this manner in two to five minutes, depending upon the size of the band and its experience with the method. "Knowing this to be true, we don't begrudge the time taken by the routine. With the visual tuner turned on before rehearsal, we find students checking themselves; they expect the routine and want to be seated as quickly as possible.

"The tuning can be competitive in yet another way. Our junior and senior high school bands are scheduled in two successive periods. Since the bands are nearly the same size, they compete against each other. The daily tuning time for each band is recorded and the time compared. The junior high band is proud when it 'beats' the senior high band and this happens often enough to make the competition interesting." [2]

Tuning by Triangulation

Nilo Hovey suggests a routine called "tuning by triangulation": "An even more accurate check on intonation will be possible if each performer hears his general pitch from three angles instead of one. In groups of wind instruments, the concert Bb chord is best for preliminary tuning because it involves the open (1st position) notes of most of the brasses, and provides the opportunity to check both the 'long' and 'short' tones of the woodwinds.

"Each section of the band should cross-tune against the Bb of the full band. In the case of the clarinets, for example:

	1st player	*2nd player*	*3rd player*
1st check:	E	G	C
2nd check:	C	E	G
3rd check:	G	C	E

"In the case of alto saxophones (two players):

	1st player	*2nd player*
1st check:	G	B
2nd check:	B	G
3rd check:	B	D
4th check	D	B

---

[2] James S. Conlee, "Competitive Tuning," *The Instrumentalist*, XXI, 4 (November, 1966), 65.

"In the case of the trombones:

	1st player	*2nd player*	*3rd player*
1st check	D	Bb	F
2nd check:	Bb	F	D
3rd check:	F	D	Bb

"All this is by no means a daily routine. It is however, a device for occasional use to encourage careful listening on the part of the band members." [3]

Effective Non-written Warm-up Exercises

Following are some variations that can be pursued to further the warm-up time without re-repeating the simple warm-up scale.

Plan A: A scale in whole notes, start *piano, crescendo* when ascending, *decrescendo* when descending.

Plan B: A scale starting *forte* at the bottom, *decrescendo* when ascending, *crescendo* when descending.

Plan C: A scale with four quarter notes on each scale step—*legato*.

Plan D: Combined plans A and C—four quarter notes starting *piano* at the bottom, *crescendo* while ascending, *decrescendo* while descending. The ensemble should get one degree louder on each scale step—not *crescendo* on each of the four quarters—each group of four remains at one dynamic level.

Plan E: Combine plans B and C—four quarter notes on each scale step starting *forte, decrescendo* while ascending, *crescendo* while descending.

Plan F: A scale with four *staccato* quarter notes on each step.

Plan G: Plan D with *staccato* quarter notes.

Plan H: Plan E with *staccato* quarter notes.

---

[3] Nilo W. Hovey, "Tuning by Triangulation," *Selmer Bandwagon*, VIII, 4 (December, 1960), 6.

Plan I: A scale with four *staccatissimo* quarter notes on each step.

Plan J: Plan D with *staccatissimo* quarter notes.

Plan K: Plan E with *staccatissimo* quarter notes.

Plan L: A scale with four quarter notes on each step with—

1. *crescendo* on the first group, *diminuendo* on the second;
2. *diminuendo* on the first group, *crescendo* on the second;
3. *crescendo* on first group, *subito piano, crescendo* on the second group, *subito piano, crescendo* on the third, etc;
4. *diminuendo* on first group, *subito forte, diminuendo* on the second group, *subito forte*, etc.

Plan M: A scale with four quarter notes having varying degrees of articulation—

1. first group *legato,* second group *staccato;*
2. first group *tenuto,* second group *legato;*
3. first group *staccato,* second group *staccatissimo;*
4. first group *tenuto,* second group *legato,* third group *staccato,* fourth group *staccatissimo.*

Plan N: Combining plan A and B with M—

1. first group *legato,* second group *staccato;*
   a. start *piano, crescendo* when ascending, *decrescendo* when descending;
   b. start *forte, decrescendo* when ascending, *crescendo* when descending;
2. first group *tenuto,* second group *legato;*
   a. start *piano, crescendo* when ascending, *decrescendo* when descending;
   b. start *forte, decrescendo* when ascending, *crescendo* when descending;
3. first group *staccato,* second group *staccatissimo;*

a. start *piano, crescendo* when ascending, *decrescendo* when descending;

b. start *forte, decrescendo* when ascending, *crescendo* when descending;

4. first group *tenuto*, second group *legato*, third group *staccato*, four group *staccatissimo;*

a. start *piano, crescendo* when ascending, *decrescendo* when descending;

b. start *forte, decrescendo* when *ascending,* *crescendo* when descending.

Plan O: Perform Plans C through N using eight eighth notes rather than four quarter notes.

Plan P: Scale patterns—

1. thirds—do mi re fa mi sol etc.

2. tonic arpeggio

3. filled thirds—do re mi re mi fa mi fa sol etc.

4. interrupted scale—do re mi fa re mi fa sol mi fa sol la etc.

Plan Q: Chord progressions—

Chord progressions can be a meaningful and productive way for warming up and tuning up the band.

There are several published works specifically designed for this type of procedure. It may be greatly beneficial, however, not to have the bandsmen reading off a score during this time.

It is an established fact that the eyes tend to cloud the efficiency of the ears. Many people believe that when a person goes blind his other senses become more acute. It is not that they become more acute, it is merely that they become more aware of the other senses. Try an experiment: blindfold yourself and let someone lead you around your home. You will be able to tell when you are led through a doorway even if you do not touch the door frames. You will be able to hear the different noises of the house reflecting off the closed-in sides. You will be able to tell when you are in the living room because outside noises are absorbed by stuffed furniture. Also, you will know where you are by the "feel." This is especially true if you are led out of the tile-floored kitchen into a carpeted living room.

All this merely points out that if the bandsmen are released from using their eyes to *read* the chords they might have more time to *hear* the chords. This is not to imply that printed materials are not to be used. On the contrary these are a great aid and can be a great training device if time is available.

When first approaching this perhaps only two different chords would be used—a *tonic* and a *dominant,* then return to the *tonic.* These chords would merely be treated as though each one contained a *fermata* above it.

The directions for playing these chord progressions can be given several ways:

1. Write the solfeggio syllables on the board.
2. Write the scale step numbers on the board.
3. Write the basic notes to be used on a staff on the board.
4. Mimeograph the groups of notes and paste them in the concert folio.
5. Give them orally.

The above suggestions must also be accompanied by instructions as to which instruments are to play which set of notes.

Illustration 4-1 is an example of what syllables would be written on the board.

do	re	do
mi	sol	mi
sol	ti	sol
do	sol	do

ILLUSTRATION 4-1

All persons playing the first parts (first clarinet, first cornet, first flute, etc.) would play the top notes; all persons playing second parts would play the second set of notes; all third or tenor parts would play the third set of notes, all bass instruments including third trombones would play the bottom group of notes. Other combinations could be used, i.e., alto saxophones on the "alto" part. All trombones could be used on the "tenor" part (third group of tones), etc.

Illustrations 4-2, 4-3 and 4-4 give some examples of four-note chord progressions that can be used in the aforementioned context. Needless to say, the group would have to be taught to

ILLUSTRATION 4-2

ILLUSTRATION 4-3

ILLUSTRATION 4-4

transpose their particular tones. The notes that would be given would be in concert pitch.

Plan R: Psychological warm-ups—

This is a very complicated type of warm-up for the director but not so for the bandsmen. It is an exercise for the director and the proficiency of his conducting technic. It does, however, serve as an excellent exercise for the bandsmen in following the baton. A complete description of "psychological conducting" is contained in *The Modern Conductor* by Elizabeth A. H. Green. Basically, psychological conducting is defined as "the process of getting a group of singers or players to respond, on a single pitch throughout, to the messages it receives from the conductor's hands and baton alone. The group has no music to read and the conductor announces nothing. The terminology implies a transfer of ideas from the conductor's mind to the performer's mind through the medium of correct and precise conductorial technic without the use of verbal directions or written notation." [4]

Illustration 4-5 gives some examples for the conductor. These can be made more difficult by adding dynamics. Changes can be made gradually or as though there were some *subito-fortes* or *subito-pianos* here and there.

So that the first attempts will not be a total failure, start very simply by varying the speed within the routines like those discussed under Plans A, B, and C. Plan C can then be used with varying numbers of quarter notes on each scale step. Simply tell the band to play continuous quarter notes on each scale step until a downbeat is given. The downbeat would indicate a move up to the next scale step. Thus the tonic might contain a ⁴⁄₄ beat, the supertonic a ⁶⁄₄, back to a ³⁄₄ on the mediant, etc., making the eighth scale step a whole note with a fermata. As the conductor becomes more proficient, add a ²⁄₄ measure and maybe eventually a ¼. A next step might be using four quarter notes and indicating

---

[4] Elizabeth A. H. Green, *The Modern Conductor* (Prentice-Hall, Inc., Englewood Cliffs, New Jersey, 1969), 231.

ILLUSTRATION 4-5

different styles of articulation, i.e., one group of *legato* tongued notes (perhaps the first three scale steps), then *staccato* for a few groups, etc. Next move to alternating a measure of ¼ quarter notes and a measure of ¼ with eighth notes. It is best to write out anything that is the least bit complicated. Remember that the last beat of the previous measure determines to the greatest extent what is to come next, i.e., the last beat—whether it is ¾, ⅝, or ¼—must be an upbeat that is clearly defined.

Outline for Warm-up Scale Practice

Illustration 4-6 is an outline that might be followed so that with an extended warm-up period many of the varying scales could be worked through within a semester.

Week	Largo MM 40–60	Adagio MM 66–76	Andante MM 76–100	Allegro MM 120–168
1st	Bb	. . .	. . .	. . .
2nd	Bb*	Bb	. . .	. . .
3rd	Eb	Bb*	Bb	. . .
4th	Eb*	Bb	Bb*	Bb
5th	F	Eb*	Eb	Bb*
6th	F*	F	Eb*	Eb
7th	Ab	F*	F	Eb*
8th	Ab*	Ab	F*	F
9th	C	Ab*	Ab	F*
10th	C*	C	Ab*	Ab
11th	Chromatic	C*	C	Ab*
12th	Db	Chromatic	C*	C
13th	Db*	Db	Chromatic	C*
14th	G	Db*	Db	Chromatic
15th	Db	G	Db*	Db
16th	Gb	G*	G	Db*
17th	Gb*	Gb	G*	G
18th	G*	Gb	Gb*	D
19th	D*	D	Gb*	Gb
20th	B	D*	D	Gb*

* That scale in thirds and tonic arpeggio.

NOTE: MM 40 could be done in half notes at MM 80 or MM 120. Likewise MM 120 could be done in eighth notes at MM 60.

ILLUSTRATION 4-6

five

Bringing Out the Band's Best Tone Quality

Intonation is the key factor when considering the quality of sound produced by a band. Any ensemble, even though it might have many fine musicians in it, will have a poor sound if they are not playing in tune with each other.

At band contests adjudicators sometimes may not score as heavily as they should against a group's poor tone or intonation, but often their findings will be reflected in the final score. Concert audiences are often affected by poor intonation although they may not recognize it as such. Often when an audience complains the band is too loud, what they are really saying is that the band was badly out of tune.

The quality of sound that emanates from a band is determined by (1) the quality of sound being produced by individuals within the organization, (2) the director's concept of the type of sound he wishes to create, and (3) how well the group is in tune.

The overall sound that the band director creates is dependent to some extent upon the organization's instrumentation. However, the discussion at hand is not "type" of sound but "quality." There should be a differentiation in regard to the words "type" and "quality" of sound. Chapter 1 discussed the various types of band sounds—not implying that one is better than the other but that each has a characteristic unique to itself. Even bands containing the same type of instrumentation can be made to sound different depending upon the director and his blending and balancing of the various sections. There should also be a differentiation between the "characteristic sound" of a particular group playing for a particular conductor and the different type of sounds that are or should be determined by the style or character of the composition being played. What may be considered a good sound for one type of composition does not necessarily benefit the rendition of another. The sound of the band during the playing of the "Chicago Tribune March" by Chambers must be considerably different than that used when playing the Pastoral and Nocturne in the *Serenade for Band* by Persichetti. There is, however, a basic quality within this "ensemble sound" that must remain constant.

Tonal consistency within the section of a band is of the greatest importance to the overall effect. There must be not only a blending of the flutes with the clarinets when they are playing together or the trombones and baritones when called upon to perform a melody line in unison but also a blending of the instruments within the various sections. To assume that all flutes will sound alike is erroneous. To assume that all the cornets in the cornet section will sound exactly alike is also erroneous. But, for the band to produce a totally unified sound they *must* sound alike. When a section is played as a whole there must be no soloists. Each must adjust his tone quality to fit in with the others. No one player should have a tone that stands out above the rest (or below the rest) in regard to quality. A single bad sound in an otherwise fine-sounding section is like adding a drop of kerosene to a kettle of soup. A fine-sounding band can only be achieved if the various sections blend with each other and the various individuals within the sections blend with those in their section.

The tuning routines described in Chapter 4 are excellent for aiding individuals and sections in creating a totally unified and blended effect within their particular sections.

Perfecting Ensemble Tone

The key to a good ensemble tone is often in the hands of the conductor. Given a group in which all individuals are capable of producing a good quality sound one would assume the organization would naturally produce a good tone. This is generally not the case. It is at this point that the rehearsal technics of the director are most important. His ability to blend and command the group to bring out the various colors in such a way that the ideas of the composer are carried out should make the final result a good performance. The director must always insist that a good ensemble tone be used throughout the entire rehearsal so that it becomes a habit with his organization.

There are many characteristics of a good band tone. Among them are clarity, compactness, sonority and resonance. A good band tone comes from an organization which realizes that a *fortissimo* or a *pianissimo* does not mean play your loudest or softest but is merely an indication of the composer's desire that the total dynamic output at a particular point should be relatively high or low, whichever the case may be. One must never ignore blend and tonal balance.

Getting first, a proper balance of volume among the players of each section, and second, a proper blend among all the sections is one of the most productive technics that can be done to achieve good ensemble sound. The band should sound like a single unit or instrument. Each individual must blend his tone to the requirements of his section, each section must blend according to the dictates of the director, who in turn must interpret the composer's intent.

The conductor who can transmit to his band the concept that

a dark color is as possible at any volume level as is brilliance has achieved something that will contribute greatly to the sound of his group.

E. C. Moore has set down, from the standpoint of the individuals within the band, twelve items that go into producing a good basic tone quality:

1. To secure a beautiful tone quality and precise intonation, the student must be taught to HEAR himself and others around him as he plays. . . .
2. Each student must be taught to rely on his own ears, not those of the director.
3. Each student must develop the sensation of SINGING through his instrument.
4. Each student must be taught how to tune his instrument properly.
5. Good posture and correct hand and head positions have a decided effect and influence upon both tone quality and intonation.
6. Good tone is supported by an adequate breath pressure, hence the necessity for breathing correctly.
7. Playing with a loose, flabby embouchure is detrimental to tone and intonation.
8. Flutists often play with lips too tense and a lip plate placed carelessly on the chin. Lifting the chin tends to raise the pitch; lowering the chin tends to flatten the pitch. The opening between the lips (aperture) must be small and narrow. Breath must travel between the lips at great speed to give "center" or "body" to the tone.
9. The oboe can be played in tune only when the reed is adjusted correctly and a proper amount inserted into the mouth.
10. When the embouchure is too relaxed, clarinetists play with poor tone quality and flattened pitches. When reeds are too soft, there may be a tendency toward flatness. The amount of the mouthpiece placed in the mouth has a definite effect upon tone quality and in-

tonation. The mouthpiece must never be allowed to wobble in the mouth. The throat should be kept open, never squeezed or constricted. A good instrument fitted with the proper mouthpiece and reed suited to the player's need is a prime requisite for producing a beautiful "in-tune" tone.

11. When brass players "puff" the checks, play with flabby embouchures, and keep "gasping" for breath, tone quality and intonation suffer. Incidentally, how can a cornetist produce a good tone when he sits "slouched" down in the chair, with legs crossed, pointing the bell of the instrument at the floor?

12. Students should be taught to control the emission of tone and play with correct intonation at moderate-to-loud dynamic levels before attempting to control the *pianissimos.* Full and resonant tones are not to be confused with loud rough ones, nor soft intense tones with weak and timid ones.[1]

How to Improve Clarinet Intonation

The prime requisite of a good clarinet section is good quality instruments plus proper reeds that are in good repair and proper adjustment. Many times an experienced player tends to use a stiff reed. It is indeed difficult to make a pleasing, flexible, sensitive tone quality with a stiff reed. It lacks the proper vibrating qualities. Therefore students should be encouraged to use a softer, more flexible, vibrant reed.

The next consideration is embouchure. When too little of the mouthpiece is taken into the mouth the reed does not vibrate properly. Students often do not grip the mouthpiece of the soprano clarinet firmly enough, while the alto and bass clarinetists often grip the mouthpiece too firmly, causing a pinched or strangled sound. In either case the sound is difficult to control.

A good clarinet embouchure *must* be one in which the flesh

---

[1] E. C. Moore, *The Band Book* (Kenosha, Wisconsin: G. Leblanc Corp., 1963), 7.

immediately below the red of the lip is kept tight against the teeth. A wrinkled chin can never produce a good tone quality or play in tune. It is absolutely necessary to play with a "pointed" chin. High tones especially are adversely affected by the bunched-up chin.

It is very important to emphasize the need for legato playing. The clarinetist often gets involved in the process of playing fast scale and trill passages and forgets about sound. Even fast notes need good sound.

Importance of the Contrabass Clarinet

Alfred Reed in *The Balanced Clarinet Choir* points out the importance of the contrabass clarinet. "The low tones of the string bass, Bb contrabass clarinet, contrabassoon and tuba produce not merely a low musical sound, but also one very rich in overtones, those upper harmonic partials of the fundamental sound actually being sounded. We know that any vibrating string or column of air will produce not only its basic or fundamental tone, but also a whole series of so-called natural harmonic overtones, simultaneously with the fundamental. It can also be demonstrated that although any tone, high or low, will produce overtones, the lower the fundamental tone is, the stronger and richer will be the overtones it produces.

"These strong overtones produced by the lower instruments in the band, actually reinforce the tones of the middle and higher instruments playing the upper notes of the chord erected on the bass tone played by the bass and contrabass instruments. This forms the sound acoustical basis for doubling the bass in octaves. Since the octave is the first (and strongest) overtone, the contrabass instrument, playing the bass tone in the lower octave, is actually sounding the 'real bass' or fundamental: whereas the bass instrument, playing the bass tone an octave higher, is being strengthened by the first harmonic (sounding an octave higher) or the contrabass instrument playing the bass tone an octave lower. The result of all this is a powerful, rich, sonorous tone, serving as the absolute foundation of the music erected above it. In the case of the B-flat contrabass clarinet (and the entire clarinet family for that matter), although the first overtone is missing, the octave is generally reinforced by different tones produced between the fundamental and various overtones in the contrabass tone." [2]

Three Steps to Quality Flute Intonation

The first places to look to improve the tone of the flute section are: (1) pad seating, (2) position of the blow-hole, (3) size of the aperture.

Properly seated pads are a critical factor in the flute section tone quality, especially when playing from first space F downward. These notes at best are weak, and are well-nigh impossible if there is even a microscopic air leak between the pad and the tone hole rim. Poorly seated pads also prevent flutists from playing soft in the extremely high register. Too often the flute section can be expected to play soft in the low register and loud in the high register and, of course, medium gray in the middle. After checking all the flutes in a section to see that they are in A-1 condition, the next place to look is at the embouchure—in particular as to position of the blow-hole and size of the opening in the lip.

One of the first things a clinician looks at is the opening in the lips. Generally young flutists have an opening far too large. This means that a large amount of air is being wasted. The air cannot be directed properly into the instrument in an efficient manner. This also prevents the flute section from playing phrases of any length. They must constantly break phrases to breathe.

---

2 Alfred Reed, *The Balanced Clarinet Choir* (Kenosha, Wisconsin: G. Leblanc Corp., 1955), p. 6.

Long tone exercises and harmonics are an aid in improving this situation.

The relationship of the lip to the blow-hole is an important factor in directing the air blown into the flute. This next item can immediately change the quality of sound being produced by the flute section. The lip *must* cover from ¼ to ⅓ of the blow-hole. The lip actually covers the hole. The lip *does not* lie beside the blow hole, it covers it slightly. A flute player should be able to feel the lip slightly projected into the hole—not pushed into the hole, but simply projected slightly over the near edge. This may mean that the embouchure plate does not rest in the curvature of the chin. It is true the flute embouchure plate is designed to fit comfortably into the curvature of the chin but if a person has long lower teeth, or a long chin, it will have to be positioned differently. Many hours spent playing long-noted, slurred scales in front of a mirror can do wonders for the flute tone. The student should concentrate on a tiny aperture and covering of the blow-hole.

Double Reed Section

The reed, which is an important factor in the tone quality of the clarinet ensemble, is the *crucial* factor for the double reeds. All the discussions about embouchure, quality equipment in A-1 condition, good breath support, control and correct styles of articulation are all for naught without a good reed.

Of the times this author has judged solo-ensemble and band contests, the oboes, by far (of the woodwinds), are the worst. A speculative guess would be that in about 95% of the cases the problem lies with the reed.

Many times a band director will ask if an adjudicator will penalize them because of the oboe player. The answer is usually: "No, I don't think so." Generally, an adjudicator does not penalize the entire band because of one erring member.

The solution to this problem is really quite simple. When a

student first begins talking about learning to play the oboe he must also know he has to make his own reeds. When he comes to the band office to pick up the instrument, his credentials for being allowed to take the instrument home would be his possession of a reed-making kit and instruction book.

There is a way of securing oboe reeds (besides making them yourself) that can prove quite adequate. If there is a professional orchestra in the area, the oboe players probably would be willing to supply reeds to the oboe players in the band. These, however, will have to be adjusted to fit the particular child's embouchure and instrument. This is another crucial factor—the reed must match the embouchure and instrument of the player. A reed that works beautifully on one instrument will not respond similarly on another. A reed that works well for one player on one instrument will not necessarily work the same for another playing on the same instrument. Unfortunately, simply walking into a music store and purchasing an oboe reed will, at best, work well only two or three percent of the time (if that much).

There are a number of books describing the methods for making oboe reeds. Having a child make his own reeds can be looked at as a hobby. A high school student does not have to have someone teach him how to make model airplanes. He buys a kit with some instructions and goes at it. Perhaps he gets help from time to time from his father, but he does it on his own. Making oboe reeds can be approached in the same way. The teacher in this case should merely help the student decide on the kind of reed needed. A good record album of a fine oboe player would challenge the student to build his reeds to sound like the recording. There are many ramifications to this, but it is a starting point.

There is one other possible source of oboe reeds. The classified ads in some professional magazines like *The Instrumentalist* have information on where handmade reeds can be secured. These are usually very high in quality. They too, however, need some adjusting to fit a particular instrument.

As for the bassoons, although individually they have about the same problems as the oboists, because of their part in the band they are no real problem. Even if they have a very poor sound their basic tone quality is easily absorbed into the fabric of the lower brass.

The immediate solution to the oboe problem is to cross-cue whenever there is an exposed part. The usual substitute is a muted cornet. However, one might experiment with the use of an E-flat soprano clarinet or a soprano saxophone on exposed oboe soli. If the band director is concerned about judges' comments, simply make a note on the score that this is to be performed by another instrument—thus penalties usually will not be incurred. It is embarrassing to be conducting and have everyone cringe each time the oboe begins playing a solo or exposed passage. If the quarterback on the football team is not successfully carrying out his assignment, the coach, no matter how short-handed, would not hesitate to switch him to another less important position and maybe use a man from the right or left end as a quarterback.

Saxophone Intonation

Larry Teal in his superb book, *The Art of Saxophone Playing,* gives a complete and authoritative discussion of all aspects of playing this instrument. The book should be on the required reading list for every band director. In this book Mr. Teal states that the saxophone is probably capable of producing more variety in tone quality than any other wind instrument. It is an instrument of great flexibility, and the tone produced is radically influenced by: (1) tonal concept, (2) reed and mouthpiece, (3) the respirator organs, and (4) embouchure.

Mr. Teal notes the importance of the oral cavity, the throat, and the lungs, all of which are vital contributors to tone quality.

He states the following: "In addition to supplying the reed with the necessary pressure to make it vibrate, they also furnish a very important resonance chamber. The bottleneck in the utilization of the chest cavity as a resonance chamber is the throat. If one observes the traffic pattern on a busy highway when it is suddenly reduced to one lane, it is easy to see that while there is a great amount of pressure on one side, only a trickle of cars leaves the point beyond the obstruction. A similar situation exists when the wind instrument tone is hampered by a tight or constricted throat. Both the pressure of the air stream and the vibrations from the resonance chamber are stifled.

"The normal, quite open position of the throat is one of relaxation, but this position is easily influenced by any unusual condition, such as nervousness (from which we get the expression 'choked with emotion') or tension. A completely relaxed approach to tone production is the first requirement for playing with an open throat, with the open position assumed similar to that followed by whispering the word 'ah.' Speaking the same word utilizes the vocal chords, which must tighten slightly to produce the sound." [3]

Aids to Brass Tone Quality

The mouthpiece is of prime importance to good tone quality on brass instruments. It has been found that a band director can quickly improve the tonal consistency of each section by having the players match mouthpieces. Generally a shallow cup will improve the production of the upper overtones and a deep cup will improve the production of the lower overtones. The choice will depend upon the tone quality desired by the band director. The shallow cup is said to produce a bright tone and a deep cup

---

[3] Larry Teal, *The Art of Saxophone Playing* (Evanston, Illinois: Summy-Birchard Co., 1963), 46.

a dark tone. To some degree this same difference may be produced by using a small throat opening or a large throat opening.

The bore of the instrument has a decided effect on the tone quality. The length of the instrument determines its pitch but the bore size affects the tone quality. The tonal consistency of each section can be improved by having the players use matching instruments.

In order to have a consistently good tonal quality, each student must have a conception of what constitutes a good characteristic sound for his instrument. It is important for the band director to create an environment where the student can listen, compare and discriminate between different tonal qualities. If a student can hear a good solid tone, he and his classmates will make faster progress. If a student can produce a satisfactory sound he can quickly take care of pitch changes.

Embouchure and wind chamber are two things a student can control within his own physical being. In embouchure we are more concerned with the lip tissues than with the muscles which make changes in the embouchure. As was stated earlier, the shallow cup of the mouthpiece and a small throat opening will enhance the production of the upper overtones. A thin embouchure likewise affects the upper overtones, and a thick embouchure affects the lower overtones as does the deep cup and the large throat opening.

In rereading the above, it can be seen there are three things which can affect tonal quality. Two items are controlled by the individual; only one affects the instrument. Most musicians have known instrumentalists who were forever seeking the instrument or mouthpiece that would do the job for them. It has been shown that tonal conception is of far greater importance than either the mouthpiece or the instrument. Any student who is receiving instruction and learning is bound to advance more quickly than a student who has the finest instrument but just sits back and waits for the instrument to do the job for him.

Blending the Percussion Section

All too often the tone emitted from the percussion section is merely a loud boom or a dull thud, accompanied by a resounding and occasionally nerve-shattering crash of the cymbals. As in the case of the woodwinds and brass and individual instruments, the percussion instruments must blend in with the rest of the band and be an integral part of the total picture. Many drummers feel, for example, that a note on the cymbals is a solo or that the bass drum merely puts out a steady boom-boom-boom-boom from the beginning of the march to the last "stinger." In reality, even in a march the bass drum should be more of a Boom-boom Boom-boom and be alternated to perhaps a BO-om-boom-boom BOOMMmmmmmmm on occasion. How often does a drummer or for that matter a band director take time to be sure the triangle is producing the proper type of sound for a particular phrase in which its tone is called for? One might ask with raised eyebrows: "A triangle produce a proper type of sound?" Doesn't the drummer just jingle the beater at the rhythmic pulse indicated on the score? Isn't that all there is to it? An emphatic NO! The player of the triangle is NOT just a jingler of a light tinkling sound. It too must blend with the other instruments playing and suit the character and style of the composition at any given point.

There is not space here to discuss the tone quality of all the members of the percussion family, but I will touch on four of the more prominent ones. The reader is referred to further sources such as the book by James Salmon entitled *The Percussion Section of the Concert Band,* published by Hal Leonard, or Kenneth Mueller's *Teaching Tonal Percussion,* published by Parker Publishing Company.

Getting the Right Sound from the Bass Drum

The bass drum in the hands of an expert *is* a musical instrument. It can produce different types of sounds or effects and can be played in such a way as to actually enhance the flow of the musical line—not just put out a rhythmic pulse. Through study, experimentation *and* practice, drummers can learn how to make different types of sounds and not just produce a constant dull roar.

Some of the factors that determine the production of sound on the bass drum include: (1) the tension of the head, (2) the spot at which it is struck, (3) the type of stroke used, (4) the type of beater used, and (5) the degree of dampening.

To determine the amount of tension each head should have, most authorities agree on the following: the batter head should be tuned to the first line *G* on the bass clef or the *F* below, and the non-batter side a major second lower.

The bass drum should not be consistently struck in the center of the head. The tone at this spot is very dull and lacks resonance. The best all-round spot is approximately six to eight inches in from the center or from a third to half way between the center and the rim.

The playing spot should vary, depending upon the style of the composition, the length of the tone desired, the volume, the quality of sound called for by the composition and the direction, flow or position of the beat within the melodic line. Generally, when striking the head near the center the tone is short. The closer the rim is approached, the longer the tone will last. For soft, legato passages a large, soft beater should be used near the rim. For staccato or quick passages a small, hard beater should be used near the center of the head. Staccato passages are more clearly delineated if the batter head is dampened.

The motion used in striking the bass drum must be neither an extreme glancing blow nor a direct hammer-like action. Some compromise between the two is most desirable. Under ordinary playing conditions it must be struck in an arc-like manner, using the arm as well as the wrist followed by an instant rebound. For special effects like the beginning of the *Allegro* section of *Chester Overture* by William Schumann, the drum would be hit dead center with a direct hammer-like action and deadened immediately.

On the subject of dampening the bass drum, Joel Leach has written: "In the concert idiom, a 'round sound' is demanded of the low brasses, so the bass drum should match this type of sound. One exception might be in a march where many directors want a well-punctuated beat which can be achieved as mentioned below.

"It is not recommended to install any type of damping device on or in the concert bass drum. In this respect, one should follow the example set by the orchestral bass drummer when he uses the drum for full, resonant, single note effects (undamped) but can immediately use the finger tips or palm of the free hand pressed against the head for slight damping. When further damping is needed to separate strokes which follow in rapid succession, the knee may be placed against the head lightly to absorb excess vibrations. This type of damping enables the drum to serve both functions (damped/undamped) equally well." [4]

Snare Drum Tuning

For tuning the snare drum we will turn to an authority on the subject: Jay Collins. In an article in *The Wisconsin School Musician* that was reprinted in *Percussive Notes,* Mr. Collins has the following to say on the subject:

"Both players and conductors must examine their own situation and ask, 'Are the snare drums contributing something to the

---

[4] Joel T. Leach, "Tuning Up Those Drums," *The Instrumentalist,* XX, 10 (May, 1966), 85.

sound of our music, detracting from it, or even masking some of it?' If the answer is 'Yes' to either of the last two parts of the question, it is probably a result of using snare drums which have not been properly tuned.

"If the snare drum sound is relatively low, or if the sound is loose and ringing or if it's a rattle sound, this will cause certain desirable musical sounds in the organization to be interfered with or lost entirely. This masking of sound by drums is one of the most frequently noticed percussion problems. . . .

"In general, the snare drum sound should be tight in pitch, sharp and penetrating, and of short duration. This snare drum sound will allow for rhythmic punctuation of the over-all sound without interfering with it. It will also allow for a cleaner, more precise rendition of snare drum solo and counter-rhythm parts.

"The response of the batter head when struck with the drum stick is a highly important point to consider when tuning the snare drum. It is possible to have the snare drum tuned so that the stick will bounce back off the batter head without the sound being necessarily good. This is usually a result of a batter head which is adjusted too tightly to vibrate freely. Thus, the response of the batter head to the blow from the drum stick is directly related to the freedom with which the head may vibrate.

"The batter head response should not be the same feel as one might get when playing with drum sticks on a wooden or metal table. There must be more freedom for the head to vibrate. When this freedom of vibration exists to the proper degree, the air contained within the snare drum is displaced. We refer to this volume of air as the air column. The air column should be allowed to move as a complete unit of air. For this to occur, the snare head must be free enough to vibrate so that the air column may be displaced downward in a complete unit. If the snare head is too tight to allow this downward displacement of the air column, the air will be displaced in an irregular manner causing puffs of air to come out of the air vent of the drum and then other air to immediately enter and replace what is lost. If the drum is properly adjusted, there will be only slight air to leave the drum through the air vent as the air column is caused to be displaced as a unit —slightly downward, then upward, and then into normal position. The snare head must be loose enough to vibrate against the snares, but tight enough to send the air column immediately upward against the batter head.

"It is obvious, therefore, that the response from the batter head is dependent upon the amount of freedom with which the head may vibrate while still being tight enough to give immediate response and help create a good high pitched sound. In addition, however, the response is related to the manner in which both the snare and batter heads are allowed to vibrate in symphathy with themselves and each other. . . ."

Mr. Collins states that through much trial and error he formed the conclusion that the snare head must be adjusted slightly tighter than the batter head. He found substantiation for his view from another percussionist in a drum publication (Louis Bellson's *Introduction to Percussion,* Vol. I. Hollywood: TRY Publishing Co., 1965).[5]

An important factor in snare drum playing is the evenness with which rhythm is played, not only as regards to tempo but also to weight of the left as opposed to the right hand sticking. A series of steady eighth notes in some cases should sound absolutely uniform—no one louder than the other or higher pitched than the other. No matter what size sticks are used they must be of equal weight and temperament to achieve an evenness of sticking. Simply purchasing a pair of sticks having the same size number does not assure that they will be exactly the same to the degree a discerning musician would desire. If one stick is heavier than the

---

[5] Jay Collins, "Tuning the Snare Drum," *The Wisconsin School Musician,* February, 1965.

other, even to a minute degree, it can adversely affect the quality of a performance, especially when trying to achieve an effectively smooth roll.

To check a pair of sticks, they should first be rolled along a flat surface to see that they are not warped. Next, they should be struck upon a hard object like the surface of a table to see what pitch sound they produce. It is amazing how different two sticks of the same size can sound. Obviously, for best results in playing they should sound exactly alike in every respect.

Cymbals: Producing a Clear Sound

Crash cymbals should never be played by striking them directly together, i.e., "head-on." They should always be played with a glancing stroke. Also, it is best to hold one cymbal steady and strike it with the other. Do not move both cymbals together! Usually the left cymbal is raised to chin or eye level and held at a slight angle (tilted to the right about 10 or 15 degrees). The right hand, during the stroke, approaches the stationary cymbal from a lowered position with the moving cymbal's uppermost edge coming in contact with the stationary cymbal and then moving on by in a follow-through. If it is to be a ringing sound, both cymbals should be raised above the head after the follow-through. If it is to be a short sound, i.e., a quarter or eighth note, then the cymbals are brought against the front part of the shoulders to choke the sound. In a situation like a march in which the cymbal plays every beat, the elbows could be anchored at the waist, i.e., upper arms held tight against the body. The right arm is down as if forming a solid base upon which to hold one cymbal while the left makes its repeated blows glancingly. In this case, the right hand will make a small circular motion, giving a small glancing blow, a very short follow-through and back again. Occasionally, at phrase endings the follow-through would be extended to give an occasional ringing sound on what would be a tenuto quarter or eighth note. In an extremely rapid movement the top ends of the cymbals may merely have to be "clapped" together, i.e., if the circular motion cannot be done fast enough.

The angle at which the right cymbal strikes the left and its speed determines the quality of sound produced as well as the dynamics. As has been mentioned before, the sound of the cymbal, like that of the other percussion instruments, must match the style of the composition, not only in dynamic level but also in quality of sound. It is possible to create a dark, glowing, velvety sound—much like a gong; or a bright, brilliant, penetrating crash at a mezzo-forte level. All cymbal crashes do not have to be a sunbright, brilliant fortissississimo calamity.

Percussionists should be advised, perhaps even coerced, to take the cymbals into a practice room and attempt to get different sounds and dynamic levels out of the "instrument." They *must not* merely CRASH them together whenever the opportunity arises.

At one band contest performance there was an incident that showed some extremely poor concepts of the use of the cymbals. The junior high school boy playing the cymbals was probably told by the director: "Watch me. Every time I point to you hit 'em together." This is just what the boy did. He would stand motionless, watching the director like a hawk. The director would point to the cymbalist, who—with both arms extended (full length) out to the sides—would bring the cymbals together with a resounding crash, closing both eyes and bending his head backward upon impact. The adjudicator, after a few such calamitous crashes, began to watch for the director's signal so he could gird himself for the oncoming onslaught of resounding reverberation.

Creating Sounds with the Triangle

Like all the instruments of the band the lowly triangle must be played in an artistic fashion and fit *into* the context of the composition.

Percussionists should have at their disposal at least two sizes of triangles—an 8-inch and a 10-inch. The 10-inch should be brought out for rather loud passages, the 8-inch for softer ones. In addition, various sizes of beaters can be used to give varying dynamic levels.

Besides the regular beater that comes with the triangle there should be a heavy, spike-size nail for heavy, loud sounds. A medium size nail file can be used when a more delicate sound is called for. A piece of wire coat-hanger size, shaped with an eyelet in one end for holding onto, makes available a light, delicate sound. It is also possible to secure various sizes of welding rods for the purpose of creating different sounds.

Producing Clear Tones with the Timpani

The timpani's tone, like that of the bass drum, is dependent upon the spot at which the drum is struck, the type of stroke used, the type of beaters used and the degree of dampening.

The concept of how the drum is struck is very important to all percussion instruments. The concept should be that the mallet is not played *into* the head but is drawn *away* from it. To get this concept across, the following idea was given this writer by George Claesgens:

> When playing the timpani, think of the head of the drum as being a very, very hot stove and the mallet as being made of very, very thin tissue paper. When the head is struck, don't burn the paper!

A common error made by snare drummers when they move over to the kettles is their execution of rolls. Rolls on the timpani must not be the buzz or bounced type used on snare drum. They must always be single stroke rolls.

six

Teaching Accurate Intonation for a Better Sound

Some of the acoustical facts that relate to the problem of intonation will be found at the opening of this chapter. Some figures will be given on these relationships, not that they will aid directly in making the band play better in tune, but to show the complexity of the problem and give an insight into why this is such a seemingly unsolvable problem. Later some ideas will be given on how various writers have made strides toward solving these problems.

The Tempered Scale

The tempered scale is of such a complex nature that perfectly accurate intonation is impossible. No instrument is absolutely in tune with the scale of the piano nor are any two makes of instruments identically in tune throughout the scale. In fact, one never hears absolutely perfect pitch.

If the piano were not tuned to the tempered scale a separate instrument would be required for each key, from seven sharps and seven flats and the key of C. The same would be true of all the instruments except the strings and the trombone.

The even tempered scale permits modulation into any sharp or flat key whatever and requires only twelve keyboard keys to the octave to do this. The disadvantages are that every tonality is a little out of tune. Each note except the key note is faulty and the major thirds, sixths and sevenths are too sharp.

The intervals of the diatonic scale are not all the same size. Normally one thinks in terms of only half steps and whole steps. There are, however, two kinds of whole steps. John Redfield in *Music: A Science and an Art* gives an explanation of these complicated frequency relationships:

"Dividing the octave into twelve equal parts sound very simple. But the person who takes up the problem expecting to find it easy will be quite likely to drop it like the proverbial hot potato. . . . To determine the notes for any diatonic scale we start with the frequency of its keynote. This we increase by ⅛ of itself; then by ⅑, $\frac{1}{15}$, ⅛, ⅑, ⅛ and $\frac{1}{15}$, of the successive frequencies. Each frequency is obtained from the preceding one by increasing the latter by some fraction of itself. . . .

"It seems then, that the increases necessary to produce the successive notes of the diatonic scale may be secured by multiplication as well as by addition. And it is increases of this multiplicative kind that have to be made in the case of our even tempered scale; only there will have to be twelve of them, and the increases will all have to be equal—multiplicatively equal. This means that we shall have to find a fraction which will double any number if that number is multiplied by the fraction twelve times. This fraction, if we could find it, would increase 1 to 2 by multiplying 1 by it twelve times. . . . To put the question into the language of the mathematician, 'What is the twelfth root of 2?'. . . . The number when we find it, correct to six decimal places, is 1.059463. Less than six decimal places are insufficient to give a rule accurate enough to tune the piano.

Comparing Frequencies

"Now compare the even tempered frequencies with the diatonic frequencies. Arranging in corresponding columns the even tempered and the diatonic frequencies for the key of A, we find their values to be as follows:

	A	B	C♯	D	E	F♯	G♯	A
Even tempered	220	246.94	277.18	293.66	329.63	369.99	415.30	440
Diatonic	220	247.50	275.00	293.33	330.00	366.66	412.50	440
Discrepancy	0	−0.56	+2.18	+0.33	−0.37	+3.33	+2.80	0

"It will be observed that the only even tempered frequency that agrees with the natural diatonic frequency is that of the keynote itself, A, and its octave. Of the remaining six notes of the scale, four are too sharp and two too flat." [1]

Just vs. Tempered and the Trumpet

By noting the numbers below it will be seen what makes for an impossible situation when it comes to building a trumpet to play in tune.

The comparative frequencies of the open tones on the trumpet and the concert pitches of the tempered scale are as follows:

	Trumpet	Tempered
C4 —	233.08	233.08
G4 —	349.62	349.23
C5 —	466.16	466.16
E5 —	582.70	587.33
G5 —	699.24	698.46

It will be noted that G4 (second line G) is 0.39 vibrations sharp on the trumpet, while E5 (4th space E) is 4.63

[1] John Redfield, *Music: A Science and an Art* (New York: Alfred A. Knopf, Inc., 1949), pp. 52–56.

vibrations flat, and G5 is 0.78 vibrations sharp. This leads one to the conclusion that G4 and G5 for the trumpet are naturally sharp pitches with G5 being more out of tune than G4, while E5 has a great tendency—over four vibrations—to be flat.

When valves are used in combinations, we have additional problems.[2]

Just Intonation

"In 'just intonation,' successive intervals between adjacent notes of the scales are actually of four kinds—not the simple whole tone and semitone to which the modern system of temperament has equalized them, but major, minor, diatonic, and chromatic semitones. Since the chromatic semitone occurs in no natural scale, let us consider the other three.

"The accurate interval between the first and second notes of the major scale is a major tone (see Illustration 6-1); the accurate interval between the second and third notes is a minor tone. The scale may be divided into two tetrachords of apparently similar but actually different construction; for the last four notes of the scale, the intervals are successively, minor tone, major tone, and semitone. It follows, therefore, that if the simplest passage be referred first to one key and then to another in the course of modulation there must be an appreciable difference in 'just intonation' between what appears to be the same interval in each scale. Thus (in Illustration 6-1) the position of the note *D* must be slightly higher in the first case (key of *C*) than in the second (key of *F*). Such a small difference is perceptible only to a trained ear, but on instruments or voices capable of performing in 'just intonation' the beauty of an untempered chord is unmistakable." [3]

---

[2] Howard Deming, "Trumpet/Cornet Intonation Problems," *The Instrumentalist,* XIII, 10 (June, 1959), 52.

[3] William D. Revelli, "Let's Tune Up!" *Etude,* June 1951, p. 22.

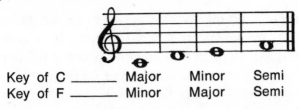

Key of C _____ Major   Minor   Semi
Key of F _____ Minor   Major   Semi

ILLUSTRATION 6-1

Dealing with Changing Temperature

In *Tuning the School Band and Orchestra,* by Ralph Pottle, another problem is pointed out that adversely affects a band's potential for playing in tune:

". . . variable temperature conditions create one of the most obstinate tuning problems confronting instrumentalists. Since 72° F. is generally regarded as normal, this is the temperature adopted for testing and tuning in U.S. factories and is the recommended level for rehearsals and concerts. But [I] found that room temperature usually rises above 72° F. at public concerts due to the multiple effects of warmth of 98.6 radiating from the audience and performing ensemble, and from heat generated by auditorium and stage lights. This increase in room temperature sharps tubas causing smaller instruments to sound flat. . . .

"In order to obtain reliable data on how a change in atmospheric temperature disturbs the tuning of a performing wind ensemble, [I] conducted an experiment in which 2640 frequency measurements of tones on wind instruments were made under various temperature conditions ranging from 60° F. to 110° F. . . .

"It was found, for instance, that a ten degree rise in temperature from 70° to 80° F.—a very common occurrence at a concert —affects the tuning of the several wind instruments by amounts which vary, generally, with the size of the instrument. For example, 69 tests on B-flat clarinets showed a mean increase in frequency of 4.3 cents. [A 'cent' is $\frac{1}{100}$ of a semitone.] . . . On cornets, 99 measurements revealed sharping by a mean of 6.2 cents. Trombones, in 18 measurements, sharped 6.9 cents, while French horns, in 48 measurements, rose 7.8 cents, euphoniums in 15 measures rose 9.2 cents, Eb Sousaphones in 54 measures rose 13 cents, and BBb Sousaphones in 81 tests revealed a rise in intonation of 14.2 cents. . . . Thus it was determined that an increase in room temperature sharps large wind instruments much more than small instruments.

"Applied to a normal concert situation, the large instruments thus govern the tuning level, because of the prominence of their bass tones and their foundational importance in the harmonic structure, despite the fact that they sharp more when temperature increases than small instruments. When players of the small instruments sense the feeling of being comparatively flat, they react in three ways:

1. They increase embouchure tension which impairs tone quality by de-emphasis of certain harmonics.
2. They develop fatigue of lips and oral cavity aggravating an already uncomfortable condition.
3. They employ all available tuning leeway to the sharp side of their instruments which disturbs the internal tuning of all wind instruments, woodwind instruments in particular. . . .

". . . findings . . . indicate clearly that when stage or concert room temperature increases, as it does in a normal concert situation, the most desirable procedure is to make correction as the concert or rehearsal progresses by adjusting the tuning of the brass basses and other large wind instruments downward." [4]

---

[4] Ralph R. Pottle, *Tuning the School Band and Orchestra* (Hammond, Louisiana: Ralph R. Pottle, 1970), 29.

How to Correct Mechanical Difficulties

Aside from the foregoing problems of the natural vs. tempered scale and changes in temperature, additional intonation problems result from such factors as faulty construction and condition of the instrument, mouthpiece and reed improperly cared for or selected, as well as lack of proper breath control and embouchure formation.

Poor quality equipment or good equipment in poor condition usually results in improper intonation. Such things as leaky pads or valves, incorrectly adjusted set screws, improperly mounted pads, worn corks (key and bumper corks on woodwinds, water key on brass), twisted posts and imperfect fittings (especially tenon and tenon receivers on woodwinds), all contribute not only to intonation problems but to poor tone quality as well.

The height of key clearance on woodwinds has a great deal to do with intonation. If a particular note like C♯4 on the clarinet is too low, removing additional cork under the key spatula will bring the pitch up. It may also improve the quality of tone for that one note. A very sharp E4 on the clarinet can be lowered by merely adjusting the height of the key just below the E/B tone hole. This may simply call for some new cork on the underside of the top half of the bridge key. Similar adjustments can be made on all the other woodwinds. It is even possible to change the size of a tone hole on a woodwind instrument. This should be done by a good repairman. A note that is unbearably sharp can be improved by simply putting shellac in the tone hole.

There is an interesting phenomenon in this regard for the saxophone family. In many, many cases it will be found that an older saxophone is a sharp saxophone. This is simply because the mouthpiece cork becomes compressed after several years of use and it is simply a matter of the mouthpiece going further on the neck, causing the instrument to be sharp.

A poor mouthpiece on an otherwise good clarinet or saxophone, cornet or trombone makes the instrument almost worthless. A mouthpiece rarely, if ever, lasts as long as the life of the instrument. This is particularly so in the case of the clarinets and saxophones. Because of the constant change in temperature, the mouthpiece has a tendency to warp. Also, the teeth eventually wear gouges in the top surface of the mouthpiece. Whenever a mouthpiece is replaced, for best results it must match the bore of the entire instrument. With brass instruments the distance the mouthpiece goes into the leader pipe can adversely affect the overall intonation.

Reeds are a great source of problems in the woodwind section. An overly stiff reed will tend to play sharp while an overly soft one may cause the tone to be flat. There are clarinetists who play successfully on soft reeds, but this is only because they can control the pitch via a firm embouchure. In many cases the reed may be soft merely because it is old. Many students play on soft reeds because when they get a good one they "play it to death." A good way of spotting an old reed is by its color. An old, soft reed is also likely to be a dirty reed.

Breath control and support are as essential to good intonation as for good tone quality. Lack of proper support of the tone usually means a generally flat pitch level. Posture too has a great effect on intonation—if only psychologically. If a cornetist's pitch level is usually flat and he constantly aims the bell at the floor, try raising the bell. Try lifting the bell of a clarinet off a player's knee if he is constantly flat, or pulling up on a saxophone neck strap.

The formation of the facial muscles which produce the embouchure is an important determining factor in the ability to achieve the proper pitch level. A loose embouchure usually causes the pitch to be flat. An overly tight one creates undue sharpness. Generally, a firm embouchure in which the flesh immediately below the red of the lip is held firmly against the teeth and a chin that is pointed downward constitutes a good embouchure. (The bassoon is an exception here.)

Besides the fact that instrumentalists must learn to adjust the pitch of any tone depending upon its position within a scale, certain notes on certain instruments, because of the fantastically complicated acoustical properties, need adjusting by the player.

The Clarinet

It has been said that if one were to improve the intonation of just the clarinet section the general intonation of the band would be improved by at least one-third. It is the clarinet section that is the largest. It is this section that not only carries the most melodic materials and lines but also does a great deal of accompanying of melodic lines being played by other sections and instruments. The clarinet section of the band can be compared in importance with the violin section of the orchestra.

The problem of getting the clarinet section in tune looms as a major task, especially when one realizes that it is this instrument that is the least flexible in regard to "lipping" or "humoring" a note to a desired pitch level.

The clarinet, like all other instruments, can be tuned mechanically in basically only one direction—downward. Fortunately most student model instruments are built to be a little sharp. This tuning is done by pulling the instrument apart at its joints. On the clarinet the first place where separation can be made is between the barrel and the upper section.

The amount of pull on any instrument must be done judiciously. The clarinet, for example, should not be pulled more than about $\frac{1}{16}$ of an inch. Any more than this will put the instrument out of balance. On the clarinet, pulling the barrel affects the throat tones considerably but has very little effect on the notes further down the instrument.

Should the clarinet be consistently out of tune in any one direction, and provided the embouchure, breath support, reed, mouthpiece, etc., are all in proper balance, it is possible to secure a different barrel length for an instrument. Most manufacturers make varying sized barrels to accommodate problems of this sort. If a new barrel is to be purchased, however, one must be certain that it conforms with the bore size of the instrument upon which it is to be used. It is also possible to have an expert repairman cut a barrel slightly if the instrument is excessively flat.

Most writers on the subject of clarinet intonation agree that the clarinet initially should be mechanically tuned as follows:

1. First, tune the second line *G* by adjusting the barrel joint.
2. Next, tune middle *C* by adjusting the middle joint.
3. Adjust third line *B* by pulling the bell.

Rarely, if ever, should any adjustment be made between the mouthpiece and barrel.

Dynamics and Intonation

There is an unfortunate tendency for all instruments to change pitch when dynamics change. The clarinetist, for example, plays flatter as he gets louder and sharper as he gets softer. The degree of flatness and sharpness increases as the degrees of dynamics approach the extremes. On woodwinds there is a tendency to decrease the pressure of the lips when playing soft and increase the pressure during *forte* playing. This is especially apparent when students do not use the proper amount of breath support.

This problem can be partially allieviated if instrumentalists are taught that it is not how hard they blow that makes the tone loud, but how fast the air is sent through the instrument. When a student is told to blow hard to play loud, invariably, in an effort to get more air into the instrument, he opens the embouchure, thus lowering the pitch. The reverse is also true; as a student tries to play softly (by using less air), he closes his mouth so that only a little air will go through. What the instrumentalist must do is not blow less air, but keep the compression the same—just blow it at a slower speed. Using this technic it will actually seem harder to play soft than loud. A much greater control of the air stream is needed for soft playing. This concept will also enable flutists to play softly in their high register.

Changing Individual Tones

The pitch of individual tones can be changed through manipulating the embouchure and breath. This "humoring" or "lipping" is the main factor that allows an individual to attain the proper pitch level for any note at any time (except the trombone —he can just move his slide a little). This humoring or lipping allows the instrumentalist to play an *E* in the key of *C* at one pitch level and *E* in the next phrase that may appear in the key of *D* at another level.

Following are the four methods by which humoring can be accomplished:

1. Increasing the pressure of the breath will result in a slight rising of the pitch.
2. Increasing the embouchure tension will result in a slight rising of the pitch.
3. Decreasing the pressure of the breath will result in a slight lowering of the pitch.
4. Decreasing the embouchure tension will result in a slight lowering of the pitch.

Altering the Pitch of the Flute

Besides the above, the flute has two additional methods by which the pitch of the instrument can be changed. By changing the direction of the air stream the flute's intonation is changed. Blowing down into the flute lowers the pitch. Blowing more across the embouchure plate raises the pitch. Many speak of this as "rolling the head joint in or out." It might be better to tell the young flutist to lower his head slightly to lower the pitch and raise his head slightly to raise the pitch. As with pulling the instrument apart at its joints to change the pitch, this too must be done in great moderation. Any drastic change from the norm will have undesirable effects. In this case, any great amount of change in the direction of the air stream will result in poor tone quality.

The Oboe: Six Adjustments

The oboe's pitch can be altered before or while playing by: (1) altering the length of the reed, (2) adjusting the length of the instrument, (3) adjusting certain pads and keys, (4) adjusting the embouchure, (5) altering the position of the reed in the mouth, and (6) through the use of added or alternate fingerings.

An oboist who finds his instrument playing flat can effectively sharpen it by either cutting off the tip of the reed or cutting the tube off slightly (by filing). Cutting the tip of the reed does, however, mean some further adjusting will have to be done on the reed's surface. Cutting a reed at the tip may also make it harder to blow.

Mechanical adjustment of an oboe that is sharp is done by pulling the tube out slightly. Once a good pitch level is found for a reed it is a good idea to put a pencil mark around the cork showing how far it should be placed into the reed socket. If a reed is pulled out more than one-eighth of an inch there may arise problems with other than the tuning note. Again, moderation is the watchword.

The pitch of the oboe can also be raised slightly by forcing the reed further into the mouth. This should be done without changing the position of the reed on the lips. The reed should not slide on the surfaces of the lips. This slight inward motion will then mean that the lips too roll further into the mouth. This puts a very slight extra bit of pressure on the reed blades, thus rising the pitch. It also makes the oboe acoustically shorter. To lower the pitch, the opposite can be done.

The Bassoon

The bassoon's pitch can be adjusted by the same means available for the oboe, except that the length of its reed cannot be changed. In addition, it can change the size of the bocal. Although bocals come in sizes 1 through 4, it is best to let an expert recommend anything other than a "1" or "2". The larger the number the longer the bocal.

Overcoming Valve Brass Problems

Valve-brass instruments have a particular problem to overcome because of a phenomenon in acoustical mathematics.

Theoretically the valves of a brass instrument are supposed to lower the pitch of the open tones one-half, one and one-and-a-half steps. If the valves are constructed precisely for this change from the open tones, any combination of more than one valve will thus be sharp. The reasons for this phenomenon are as follows (please note that the figures given below are an over-simplification of highly complicated acoustical mathematics but are so given to show in simple terms the problems involved):

The length of the cornet with no valves depressed is approximately 54 inches. In order to lower the pitch of open tones one-half step, the player depresses the second valve. The additional tubing needed to be added by this second valve is about 6¼ inches. Thus the note *G* (second line) takes 54 inches of tubing, while the note F-sharp takes 60¼ inches. It would therefore seem logical that if it takes 6½ inches of tubing to lower the pitch one-half step (by using the second valve), the first valve which lowers the pitch one whole step would have to be 12½ inches in length. Thus the note *F* (first space) is formed by an instrument that is 66½ inches in length. So it takes 6½ inches of additional tubing to lower a 54-inch cornet one-half step and 12½ inches of extra tubing to lower the 54-inch cornet one whole step.

The problem arises when we want to move one-half step lower than *F* to secure the note *E*. Although 6½ inches of tubing was sufficient to lower a 54-inch instrument one-half step, it is inadequate for lowering a 66½-inch instrument. The cornet playing the note *F* is really 66½ inches in length. It has the added length of the first valve (54-inch basic length plus 12½-inch first valve). Lowering this instrument one-half step would take a little more than 6½ inches of tubing. Thus combination "1" is in tune as is combination "2", but combination "1" and "2" are sharp.

Because of this problem a compromise is often made. In order that combination 1-2 is not too sharp, the slides are built a little flat. This does mean however that the notes *F* and *E* may now be a little flat, but combination 1-2 is not too sharp. However, there still remains a problem; combinations 1-2 and 1-2-3 are still sharp. It is for this reason, among others, that D_4 and C-sharp$_4$ on cornets are quite sharp.

Mechanical Adjustment

To make up for the different lengths of tubing needed for various valve combinations, cornets and trumpets are constructed with movable tuning slides. A trigger mechanism on the first valve and a ring on the third valve makes them instantaneously adjustable while playing. By extending the third valve slide, for example, the D_4 and C-sharp$_4$ which are normally slightly sharp can be brought down to the correct pitch level without having to adjust the embouchure.

If a player is willing to use the third value slide he can have his third slide made a little shorter than the standard length. This makes the more frequent use of the third valve possible as an alternate for the combination of first and second and corrects the E-flat and all A-flats.

Trombone

Though the trombone is capable of playing perfectly in tune, audiences and contest adjudicators will attest to the fact that this section does not achieve this "perfect intonation" any better than do other sections of the band. This is because many trombonists are led to believe that there are seven slide positions. This is a false assumption, particularly for the advanced player. The slide position is determined by the *ear*—not by the distance the arm reaches. For example, one writer on the subject, Mark R. McDunn, gives a chart showing 51 slide positions (*The Instrumentalist,* January, 1966).

Baritone and Tuba Mechnical Adjustments

Baritones and tubas are not fitted with valve slides as are cornets and trumpets, but some manufacturers do produce instruments with a fourth valve to alleviate the problems caused by improper length valve slides. As with the cornet, combinations 1 and 2 are sharp; 1, 2, 3 are sharper. The fourth valve takes the place of the 1-3 combination and the 2-4 combination takes the place of 1-2-3.

Additionally, there are compensating systems available on some baritones and tubas. The basic principle of the compensating system is that additional lengths of tubing are automatically brought into operation when certain combinations of valves are used.

A Physiological/Psychological Approach

Aural capacities of students have to be awakened so they can begin to perceive for themselves whether they have a tone that sounds in tune. Simply telling a student he is out of tune or walking him up to a strobo-tuner to watch the wheels whirl will not suffice.

Once a student has a good instrument in good repair and an embouchure that is formed properly, he may have to be taught the technics of focusing his tone to produce a good quality sound that is also in tune. The concepts to be learned are both physiological and psychological.

A step in this development of musical perception of tone has to be through aurally descriptive images. Prior to a discussion of these images, a student must be given opportunities to hear good performances. In order for a student to really understand what it means to play in tune he must hear some representative performances that are examples of the highest musical standards. If a student has ever heard a beautifully rendered performance he will more readily understand that he has a responsibility within the ensemble regarding tone and intonation. It is also necessary for students to develop a vocabulary that includes definite musical concepts.

Another step in the development of these perceptions is to have the students understand such things as chord structures, scale construction, the overtone series and dissonant and consonant harmonies, as well as the different scales, i.e., natural, tempered and just. Many students do not even realize that when playing a simple C scale they are playing some half-steps and whole-steps in specific combinations.

If a student plays with a very flat sound—not only flat in pitch but flat or anemic in quality—he can be encouraged to "think high." Usually a dull, thin or mushy tone, caused by some physiological reason (improper support, tongue too low in the mouth, poor posture, flabby embouchure, etc.), can be improved psychologically by having the student pretend he is blowing at his forehead, i.e., aiming his air stream high.

Because the student is producing a dull, thin, mushy tone he may also be producing a tone that is flat in pitch. By using description words like "dull," "mushy," "anemic," etc., the student can get a mental perception of a tone that is on the flat side. Similarly, words such as "harsh," "forced," "strained," or "pinched," would indicate a sharp tone.

Ideally, a student should aim his tone at an imaginary bull's-eye several yards away from his instrument. If the tone is harsh, strident and/or pinched, the imaginary arrow (the sound) will hit far above the mark and maybe even over-shoot the target. If the sound is mushy, dull and/or anemic, it will hit low on the target or not reach the target at all.

The harsh, strident, pinched tone will usually be sharp. The dull, anemic tone will usually be flat. The tone that is centered, i.e., focused so that it hits square in the middle of that imaginary bull's-eye, will more than likely be in tune.

Solutions to the Intonation Problem

Casimer Kriechbaum gives some basic concepts toward approaching a solution. He writes: "There are two basic concepts that will allow anyone to be able to work with confidence toward producing musical groups with good intonation.

Concept #1

Perfect intonation at all times is not possible; therefore, it is necessary to use knowledge of the characteristics of sound and the psychology of human hearing to help us to choose which intonation problems to attack and solve first. The problems most noticeable to the audience and the problems most easily solved should be the first ones worked on, since the correction of these easily heard and easily solved problems will result in immediate, obvious improvement. (Fortunately, the two catagories are largely identical, as the basic method of improving intonation is to have the performers *hear* their errors.)

Concept #2

'In tune' playing comes only when the performers know when they are in tune: not from the fine instrument; not from the excellent ear of the leader. The performers are "programmed" to play in tune—the instrument and the 'ear' of the director have relatively little bearing on the ability of the group to perform in tune.

"The list below gives those items that can help the band director choose which things should be worked on first and which things should or can be left until later.

"Intonation problems are more noticeable:

1. On long notes than short ones (including groups of short notes, fast scale passages, etc.).
2. On notes before a rest or at the end of a piece or phrase.
3. On unison passages.
4. On passages in octaves.
5. On intervals of 4ths and 5ths.
6. On imitative passages at unison or octave.
7. In thinly scored passages than tutti passages. (In this connection it should be mentioned that even in thickly scored tutti passage entrances and releases that are not together expose out-of-tuneness that would not be obvious if attacks and releases were clean.)
8. In the extreme registers of the instrument.

"These observations can be used to help intonation in several ways: initially they can act as a guide to help the director to select music that will allow problems to be worked on or in which intonation problems will not be easily noticed.

"According to this list, this would mean that music that is mostly tutti, 'moves around,' avoids extreme registers, is homophonic in texture, or avoids octave and unison passages can more easily be made to sound 'in tune' to many listeners. It will, especially if played by a large group. This kind of music is known as 'safe' music for contests.

"After the music has been chosen (either to expose or hide problems) the next step is to work on the intonation problems.

"Now: Concept #2 is used to solve these problems. A performer will play in tune (or be miserable) when he knows what 'in tune' sounds sound like and when he recognizes that all other sounds are unacceptable. The job of the teacher, therefore, is to make the student aware of what the correct sound is, then the student will play in tune (if reminded from time to time). Once students know what the 'in tune sound' is, they are extremely critical of out-of-tuneness."

The following procedure is one suggested by Casimer Kriechbaum on how to approach work on intonation during the course of a rehearsal:

"Following our above listed order of ease of noticeability, we make the intonation easier for the student (and for ourselves) to hear by picking a note from a piece. Any note will do. Have students sustain it, while the teacher says, 'Listen to that! It is terribly out of tune. How many people can tell?' Possibly some students will raise their hands. If not, repeat the note and the question. Then, if it is a triad, sing the chord to them: 1-3-5-3-1 or *Do-Mi-Sol-Mi-Do*. If unison, skip down to the procedure for unisons. Say, 'Everyone is supposed to be playing one of the notes I just sang. Can you pick yours out? No? Then play the chord again and listen to yourself; pick which note is yours.' Teacher now sings 1-3-5-3-1 again and directs everyone who has '1' to play; everyone else listens. (Some wrong notes will be played the first few times.) Comment that some people are playing wrong notes. Sing 1-3-5-3-1 again and ask the whole class how many can hear that everyone is not playing or singing the note asked for. When you get them to identify pitches wanted by sound, you then comment that the notes are not all the same (or in tune). Ask how many of the people can tell. If most or many cannot, then ask for only a specific octave or even one section to play a unison note. Again, comment that it is out of tune (it will be) and ask who can hear it. If the class still does not hear, have one student play the note, then have another student pull out his tuning slide until it is obviously flat and slowly come up to pitch. (The trombone is excellent for this.) Instruct the class to raise hands when they hear the pitches match perfectly. Someone will probably comment, 'That's fine, I can tell when they do it but I cannot tell whether I'm sharp or flat.' The answer to that is: 'You do not have to know whether yours is sharp or flat. All you have to do is know that it is not right.' The next step is to change. Logic says if you are not in tune you have to be either sharp or flat, so if you change it has to get either better or worse. If it gets better you are going the right way. If it gets worse you are going the wrong way. After a while the adjustment will be automatic and correct. This is a matter of reflex, not an intellectual problem.

"After all of this, ask for a section to play the note again. Point out the tone is 'rough' when out of tune (beats) and smooth and clear when in tune. Every time you do this, become harder to please. (It does not take long to get one tone perfectly in tune.) Next step: again add other octaves of the same tone, one octave at a time, and have students listen for beats, intonation, etc. If you cannot get octaves in tune with groups, take two individuals. Have one play one note, the other matches it at the octave. Move one up and down so the class can hear it in tune and out of tune. Have hands raised when the students think they hear it in tune.

"Next step (not necessarily the same day) is to follow this same procedure with the 5th of the chord. You sing 1-3-5-3-1. Have '1' of the chord play (in tune as above), then add the fifth. Teach the sound of the perfect fifth as you taught the sound of the unison and octave. Next step, again, probably not the same day, is to teach the sound of major and minor thirds.

"Later, you can teach 7ths of the chord. Sing 1-3-5-7-5-3-1. Follow the above procedure . . . . root-5-3, then 7th or root-5-7. Perfect intervals must be tuned first because they are the most obvious, both for performers and the audience to hear and also because there is the least room for difference of opinion. An octave or unison is unquestionably in or out of tune. A perfect 5th or 4th can be played perfectly in tune but a major or minor interval can be played in several different places and still be acceptable because of the fact that opinion is a factor in these intervals (high thirds, low sevenths, leading tone, etc.)." [5]

---

[5] Casimer Kriechbaum, "Improving Intonation in Performing Groups," *The Instrumentalist,* XXIII 7 (February, 1969), 60.

seven

Methods for Achieving
Balance and Precision

In successful organizations goals are well defined, most times in written detail—minutely defined details, and a person is charged with heading up the project. It is this person's responsibility to see that all parts of the organization so designated, work together toward the final solution of the problem or conclusion of the project. It is this person's responsibility to see that the organization's resources and expertise are properly geared in the direction of the aims as set forth by the initial goal statement. This is the position the band director is in upon taking up a new piece of music.

The band director cannot give out the music to the band members and "let them go at it." He must not only direct them with precision (in minute detail) as to tempo and when each member should come in and play his part; he must also explain how that assignment is to relate to other things that are happening. Drawing on the analogy of the men's civic club: If in fact a walkway is to be constructed along the south side, flowers can also be put in; however, the flowers must not be planted until after the walkway is in. If the flower seed is planted first, the weight of the workmen trampling the ground as they put in the walkway would no doubt bury the seeds so deep that the sun's heat cannot reach them. In the band, even though the trombones may have an interesting idea they must not produce it in such a way that the flutes cannot project their musical heads above the trombones' bass sounds.

How to Achieve Balance

A band that receives an "A" in the box on the adjudication sheet marked "balance" does not have all its instruments playing with equal balance. Good balance in a band's performance is in reality imbalance, i.e., some instruments are playing louder than others some of the time.

Possibly one of the greatest detriments to good balance (i.e., the proper amount of imbalance) in a band's performance is the dynamic levels that are placed on the score of individual parts. All too often the young musician seeing the letter *f* will play loud regardless of the part which he is playing in the fabric of the composition. There are works being published in which the composer tries to balance the various voices of the band, but the usual procedure is simply to mark *forte* or *piano* or *mezzo forte* on all the individual parts. Even when a *cresc.* appears, for good balance all instruments should not necessarily make the same degree of *crescendo*. Bandsmen must be taught that all dynamic markings are merely indications of the general level of the composition at any one point. They are *not* the exact level for each instrument.

Some composers indicate relative dynamics by marking the melody line louder and the accompaniment softer. They indicate louder levels when only a few are playing and softer levels as the numbers increase. It should be noted, however, that this is generally not the case. Most often the same dynamic marking is given to all the parts, leaving the player and the conductor the task of achieving a proper balance. Someone once questioned Brahms about instructions for the performance of a selection. He stated that if he were writing for a musician further instructions were not necessary, and if he were not, they would not help.

Sometimes students feel it would be helpful if each dynamic marking could mean a certain number of decibels. Toscanini once said: "There are a thousand *fortes,* use the one that fits." This statement will point out to any questioning student the impracticality of his request. Students must learn that balance is the responsibility of each individual. A person playing the melody must play out and the accompaniment must hold back.

The following terms, while not defined as dynamic levels, have a significant affect on dynamics:

Solo—alone, but important, above the accompaniment, hence louder.

Soli—all parts so marked are important, hence somewhat louder.

Tutti—all are playing, hence less for each individual.

Espressivo—expressively, important. Be sure you are heard, hence louder.

Dolce—sweetly, also used to identify a passage that must sing over the music, hence louder. Often misleadingly defined as sweetly and *soft.*

When instruments are sharing the same part, the level should be suggested by the weakest instrument, not the strongest. (Heed well, trumpets!)

All voices playing in the same rhythm should balance equally. This requires that the higher parts be held back and the inner voices brought forward, the stronger instruments yield to weaker ones.[1]

Which Instrument Should Be Louder?

There is a general guide one can use to decide which instruments are to be loudest and which are to be softest. Following is a list of eight items in order of their importance. Number One

---

[1] William Schaefer, "Interpreting Dynamics," *The Instrumentalist,* XXII, 4 (November, 1967), 34.

should be the loudest; Number Two, second loudest; Number Three softer yet, etc., all depending upon their position within the musical fabric.

Number 1—*f+*   (loudest) .... melody.

Number 2—*f/mf*   (loud *mezzo-forte*) . melodic harmony, i.e., a 2nd part in a duet-like passage.

Number 3—*mf*   .... counter-melody or obligato.

Number 4—*p/mf*   (soft *mezzo-forte*) .. melodic bass line.

Number 5—*f/mp*   (loud *mezzo-piano*) . after-beats (in a march however, this may be moved up in importance).

Number 6—*mp*   .... sustained harmonic parts.

Number 7—*p/mp*   (soft *mezzo-piano*) . snare drum (again, may be moved up in importance especially during the final strain of a march).

Number 8—*pp*   (softest) .... rhythmic bass (bass drum).

Much rehearsal time can be saved if the band director can go through a score to be played by the band and mark the levels like those given above and have his band librarian transfer them to the individual parts. It is also a good idea to have the bandsmen get into the habit of marking (IN PENCIL) various levels on their scores when directed to play varying degrees of dynamics. A pencil attached to or in every folder will save countless hours.

The large question that looms is: Why don't composers mark the scores themselves? Surely they know which parts are more important than others. It is true that they could, but composers cannot know the number in each band that will be playing their compositions. They cannot pre-determine the maturity of the individuals within the section. A strong player on the first cornet part will have to play softer than those who might be weaker players on the second and third parts. Seating has a decided effect upon the projection of the melody or harmony or counter-melody part. A band that rehearses on risers is at a decided disadvantage when it performs on a flat gym floor at a contest.

Diagnosing Balance Problems

Ralph Laycock has set down in outline form [2] those items that contribute to the problem of ascertaining what the balance should be at any given moment. The problems lie in four general areas: the score itself, the musical meaning, physical factors and personal factors.

A. The Score
1. Most scores indicate only a general volume, all instruments being marked identically.
2. Those that do differentiate may or may not take into account each instrument's dynamic range, so personal judgment will still be needed to assess their proper relative volume. For instance, does *forte* for middle-register flute specify the same amount of sound as does *forte* for the trumpet at the same pitch?
3. Few scores indicate the appropriate number of performers needed per section. (An entire clarinet section accompanying a flute solo will entirely cover the flute.)
4. Maturity and personality of the individual performers (of real significance in school situations) cannot be taken into account. Even the very presence of a particular instrument cannot be taken for granted.
5. Some instruments may not be specifically indicated—e.g., in Baroque music, the "realizing" of the figured bass, the presence of an additional instrument on the bass line, the doubling of string parts by oboes, etc.

---

[2] Ralph G. Laycock, "Balance," *The Instrumentalist*, XX, 9 (April, 1966), 80.

B. The Musical Meaning
1. What is (are) the most important musical idea(s)?
2. Has it been well-scored, or do "fillers" really obscure the important ideas?
3. What are the authentic performance practices? Would not the small, balanced chorus and orchestra employed by Handel give a more authentic performance than the mammoth unbalanced groups often used?

Problem of Achieving the Balance Once It Has Been Decided

C. Physical Factors
1. Lack of understanding of music by players—they do not have a full score (which some conductors seem to forget), and must be helped to a full understanding of the music.
2. Performers who, for one reason or another, do not listen as they should.
3. Inability to produce mature sound, especially in extreme registers, and with it, inability to play either a very full or a very quiet sound.
4. "Extroverts" playing powerful instruments.
5. Dependence on a few secure players to carry the group even when their parts are not important.
6. Nervousness and consequent lack of projection.
7. Type of tone—"buzzy" saxophone, "strident" trumpet, "flabby" high clarinets, etc., can make balance impossible to achieve.
8. Flexibility of tone quality—a subject of great importance to the obtaining of proper balance, and one that is not always sufficiently recognized. A brilliant tone *seems* louder than it is, a mellow tone *seems* quieter than it is, and performers often inadvertently use the one when the other would be more helpful in achieving both balance and appropriate emotional feeling.

Teaching Balance Successfully

"As with every other aspect of musical performance, the conductor will achieve better balance, and that more quickly, if he teaches his individual players to be aware of and to work constantly for this most valuable goal. The leader who does no more than tell his players, "You are too loud," "You aren't loud enough," etc., will, like the one who teaches rhythm by rote, have to do this with nearly every measure of every piece that is rehearsed. But there are many things common to various musical compositions, and as players are taught to recognize them they will, on their own, solve many of them more readily and be able to accept their instructor's counsel when needed. Good balance involves hundreds of individual judgments both as to what is needed at each instant, and as to how one must handle his instrument in order to produce exactly what is desired. This ability to so judge must be built up over a long period of time. Though it is not at all as simple step-wise or immediate, as might seem to be implied below, the gradual expansion of the students' (and even the instructor's) hearing can be guided in somewhat the fashion given below:"

Mr. Laycock's suggestions that follow can also be used in the context and as a refinement of the warm-up/tune-up segment of the rehearsal, along with add-on procedures set forth here in Chapter 4 under "Proven Tuning Routines."

"The first step must be that of learning to produce a sound exactly equal to that of one's neighbor(s). With the entire group listening, have the first and second chair players of a small section (for instance the first two cornets) each play the same note (e.g., tuning C) individually and help them (perhaps with suggestions from their classmates) to match tone, pitch, and volume as exactly as possible. Then match the second and third chair players in similar fashion, and continue to the end of the section in like pairs, so that each has a chance to feel and hear the sensation of matching his neighbor exactly, or at least as closely as he is able to. Then have the entire section play simultaneously, with each person trying to match perfectly those on either side of him. If and when it arrives (after further coaching if necessary), point out the blended and united "ensemble sound" that emerges. Repetition of the experiment, perhaps with a different type of instrument, can help reinforce the experience. Subsequently, much work, preferably in sectionals and/or in individual pairs, will be very helpful both in assisting students to gain greater control of their instruments and in learning to listen carefully for balance.

"The next step is to balance like instruments in harmony. Again in full rehearsal, use cornets, clarinets, or triply-divided (trombones) etc., to demonstrate.

"Let us suppose we are again using cornets: tune carefully, then have the thirds balance, as above, the written F. Next, the seconds on A, and the firsts on the upper C, with comments solicited from the entire organization as to what is wrong and how to correct it. Then have all three notes played simultaneously and adjusted as needed. When it 'locks in,' take the opportunity to point out the beauty and richness of the composite sound that is heard in a well-balanced sound and well-tuned group. . . .

"Now they are ready to be put together in complete families and to learn to take into account the very real differences in sound that exist between members of even the same family. Again demonstrate with the middle range of each section (a triad selected from any appropriate measure in a piece under rehearsal should be used). After tuning and balancing the notes played by each section, as above, have them each play in turn—cornets, trumpets, horns, trombones, baritones, basses, and, with the help of the class, attempt to get equal projection from each group. When successful, have all sections play together, doing the final adjusting as needed. Both they and the remainder of the group should listen intently to the sonorous result obtained, and those playing should individually check their effort and sound against the total as they hear it, so that they may gain the ability to estimate their sound relative to the whole. It is this individual responsibility for the final results that makes it possible to get something done about the problems of balance. . . .

"Similar experiments with the other major families will turn up other discrepancies in their tonal intensity (oboes and piccolos may seem loud, flutes quiet, etc.) and should drive home the point that constant listening and awareness of what is going on in the music is absolutely essential to good balance, even the 'equal' balance within which we have been working.

"Experiments involving the use of notes in the most extreme registers of the instruments will point up still other problems, some of which may be unsurmountable at the present state of maturity.

"The next and final step in achieving 'equal' balance (but only the beginning of developing the varied balance necessary in actual music-making), is to build a balanced tutti by having each family play a particular chord in turn, balancing it both internally and in total with the other 'families' of the organization."

"To reinforce these procedures the director should record the proceedings and either edit or reproduce sections that make the final point so the students can hear the 'before' and 'after'."

How to Achieve Precision

Precision in a large ensemble is dependent upon unaminously unified and accurately articulated rhythms. This totally unified action is dependent, as are all things in the band's performance, on individual prowess. This prowess must be not only in rhythm but also in articulation. Good rhythmic accuracy is not totally possible unless individuals have developed a high degree of facility in the use of the tongue for varying styles and speeds of articulation.

In the area of articulation the band members must not only be able to articulate correctly, i.e., use the correct style and proper speed, but must also be aware of the exact ictus of the sound, the length of the individual tones and the correct method and style of release. The word "ictus" is used to describe the beginning of the tone. Normally the word "attack" is used in this connection but this implies to many a forceful approach to the sound. The use of the word "ictus" may be psychologically good as it does not carry the connotation of force. Granted, the word "ictus" comes from a Latin word that means "to strike," but most students do not know this. In present day terminology it means "metrical and rhythmical stress or beat in utterance." As the "attack" or commencing of the tone is important to precision we will discuss this at some length later in this chapter.

The director must take great care in instructing his group in the length of notes in various passages. Notes not having any marks above or below are not always to be played with the same degree of attachment or detachment. It is particularly important for clarity's sake to inform the band as to how long *staccato* notes should be played. Incidentally, the word "staccato" does not mean "short." Not all notes marked with dots are to be played half their value as the definition for this term is indicated in the *Harvard Dictionary of Music*. "Staccato" merely means to "detach" or "separate." More will be said on this matter later, under interpretation.

How to Perfect Conducting Accuracy

Good precision is greatly dependent upon the conductor's accuracy of beat with his baton. The bandsmen must be able to clearly see each ictus. A clearly defined ictus shown by the baton usually results in a clearly unified starting tone by the band.

The two items that will aid in the precise beginnings include: (1) a good preparatory beat by the director, and (2) all eyes of the bandsmen on the director.

The conductor's preparatory beat and its many ramifications

are thoroughly and comprehensively discussed in a book by Elizabeth A. H. Green (*The Modern Conductor,* published by Prentice-Hall), so it will not be gone into here. All we need say here is that the preparatory beat *must* show (1) tempo, (2) dynamic, and (3) style.

An item that can help to insure the band's getting off on the right foot (correct tempo) is for the director to sing to himself the first few measures of the composition to be played. This is especially necessary with a march or some other relatively fast composition where the rhythmic flow gets going from the very first beat (actually from the preparatory beat). Many conductors fall into the habit of counting a full measure before starting, i.e., "One . . . . two . . . . ready . . . . go!" Many begin this way not because the *band* really needs this setting of a tempo but because the *director* needs it. He needs this pause for two reasons: first, because he needs to decide which tempo he is going to make, and second—perhaps unwittingly—as a disciplinary measure. All too often this technic is used because it acts as a measure for gaining the student's attention. Rather than commanding their attention with his up-raised arms, the director (in some cases) has to warn the band verbally to "come-on . . . . get ready . . . . let's - - - - go!!"

What happens in this case is that the director is verbally starting the band—usurping the duties of the baton. This in turn psychologically usurps the baton throughout the composition. Starting with the command from the baton will help to establish the authority of the stick.

Following this precise preparatory beat a clean, clear downbeat is of greatest importance. A conductor can most effectively acquire this by practicing his score in front of a mirror with a metronome going. Start the metronome and make the preparatory beat and downbeat fit with the "ticks." One might even use members of his own family as guinea pigs. Have them sing a tone on your downbeat. It is especially necessary to practice the beginning of a composition if it does not occur on the first beat of the measure.

Perhaps at this point a word should be said about the conductor's practicing. Conducting skills are motor skills, not unlike fingering a clarinet or manipulating the slide on a trombone. Just as a clarinetist and trombonist must practice, so too should a conductor practice. A rehearsal is not the place for the conductor to practice! A rehearsal is a performance for the conductor. The conductor *must* know his part because he must concentrate on the bandsmen at this time. About the only time a conductor can practice on the band is during the warm-up period (the psychological conducting items) or occasionally during a band rehearsal when he is trying for a special effect by making use of the baton only (non-verbally). This, however, should be done in context. It should not be done repeatedly without some explanation to the band members. In this connection the director should take time during the course of a rehearsal to see that his gestures are being successful, i.e., indicating to the band the way he wishes them to play. These periodic (perhaps as often as once a week) inward lookings can ultimately save many hours of rehearsal, for as the director looks inward so too will the band.

It is a good idea to have the band memorize the first few notes or measures of every composition to be played. After a few weeks of rehearsing a composition, practice starting out with all scores closed—the director's score also! Then, if the director will take a breath at the time the band members should be taking a breath all should be under way simultaneously. Incidentally, the director should breathe in tempo, style, and in-take of the amount of air he would need to play the first notes himself.

Because the bandsmen must constantly keep one eye on the director, it is of greatest importance that only two players read off one music stand for the smaller instruments and only one to a stand for such instruments as the tubas and percussion. The training of the band to watch can effectively be done during the warm-up period, especially if psychological conducting exercises are used. It might be a good practice to change tempos with a composition, even when not called for, just to exercise the director's command and the attention of the bandsmen. Doing this too often and without definite purpose is poor rehearsal psychology, however.

Good precision within the composition is greatly dependent upon the conductor's accuracy of beat with his baton. The bandsmen must be able to clearly see when each ictus begins. A clearly defined ictus shown by the baton usually results in a fairly unified rhythmic flow by the band members.

Achieving Individual Rhythmic Accuracy

Aside from the director's accuracy with his baton, the next most problematic area is individual rhythmic accuracy on the part of the bandsmen. This problem is most often overcome by rote training. This usually comes about by constant reiteration of the music over a long period of time. This, however, does not, even by average standards, solve the problem. It will improve slightly by accident but a planned program of attacking the problem is best. At best, the re-playing and re-re-playing of a problematic rhythmic area will only result in its being played with a unified inaccuracy. Often a band will play a particular area of a composition with considerable precision but rhythmically inaccurately. In other words, they play beautifully—but *incorrectly.*

Much of the precisely incorrect rendering of various areas within a composition comes about because a band is rehearsed exclusively by the "beginning to end" method. The director is just hoping it will improve—and it does, in a certain way. Many times a thing done incorrectly enough times will begin to sound correct. Among the many examples of this are the following:

The half note: Have an advanced player play from a composition that is rather slow, in ¼ meter that has a half note at the end of every four measures. Ask the band to witness the playing. See how many can detect the fact that in perhaps 99 cases out of 100, that half note will be followed by a breath, making it actually a dotted-quarter with an eighth rest. Granted, many times the half note may be the end of a phrase or period, but must there *always* be a breath after a half note that is at the end of a measure? Try it with a composition that has a whole note at the end. How many performers will play *up to* the fifth beat? More likely than not the performer will play a double-dotted-half note. Rarely will it be a *full* four beats.

For more of these typical rhythmic errors as well as a discussion of the exact length of a whole note and how these problems might be approached, the reader is referred to Chapter 3 of my book *Administering the Elementary Band,* published by Parker Publishing Company.

Terminology is also a thing that is not precisely used by many. There is no such word in the *Harvard Dictionary of Music* as "pick-up." There is such a thing in music as an "upbeat" or an "anacrusis." And, what is a "bird's-eye" or a "hold"? The precise word is a "fermata." When indicating that the band is to start at a particular place in the music, how many times has it been said, "Start in bar five"? How can a band start *in* bar five? One can start *at* bar five or *in* the fifth measure but not *in* the fifth bar. Is it "music"? No, not really. It is a "score." We often use the word "score" to refer to the conductor's score but all musicians use a "score" to play "music." "Music" is that stuff which is created by the act of blowing into an instrument while reading off a printed page—the "score."

These may seem like small, insignificant, even irrelevant items to some, but if the professional music educator is so careless with his terminology and accuracy it scares one to think about the medical profession. If they are as careless with their terminology and accuracy of prognosis as some teachers, "woe be unto" their patients.

Solving the Problem of Slow Passages

In all band literature some of the most glaring and obvious imprecisions occur in slow passages. One might mistakenly equate *slow* with *ease of playing;* not so!

Many a conductor when directing a composition with a slow choral-like section will make large, long, flowing gestures totally lacking in any point of reference for the musicians to discern the start of individual beats within the rhymic framework. This leads the bandsmen to "guess" where the ictus actually occurs. After a little practice with a baton in front of a mirror, a conductor can use his wrist to make a slight "tick" or "flick" of the baton at the exact point where each beat is to occur. This "tick" can occur within a gesture that is large, long and flowing. This subject is also covered in *The Modern Conductor* by Elizabeth A. H. Green.

Tempo Phenomenon

There is an interesting phenomenon in regard to tempo that the director must constantly be aware of and learn to reconcile between the bandsmen and his own conducting. This phenomenon has many ramifications in connection with precision:

Slow tempos tend to slow down.
Slow notes tend to slow down.
Soft passages tend to slow down.

Fast tempos tend to speed up.
Fast notes tend to speed up.
Loud passages tend to speed up.

There are many occasions in band literature when these items come into direct conflict with each other. The band is often called upon to play portions of works that contain some fast-moving notes for some sections while others are playing slow-moving notes. In the case of balancing a single melody or soli, the soli *must* play loud while the accompaniment *must* play soft. There then is the tendency for the soli to play fast and the accompaniment to play slow.

Fugal passages are great sources of hodge-podge playing. A look at rehearsal number 9 in the *Prelude and Fugue in G minor* by J. S. Bach as arranged by R. L. Moehlmann is such a case. On the first two beats of the measure (see Illustration 7-1) the flutes and clarinets are moving in eighth notes while the lower clarinets, baritones, third trombones and basses are playing half notes. Then the reverse occurs. In the second measure after 9, some have moving eighths, some have steady quarters, and a few begin the measure with an eighth and two sixteenths.

The sixteenths are probably going to be too fast, the quarters may slow down and the eighths will have a tendency to move forward, particularly with the eighth note appearing on the second half of the second beat being slurred to the eighth note figure on the third and fourth beats. Rehearsal number 10 (Illustration 7-2) has a drastic example of the fast-moving notes in juxtaposition with slower ones. The English horn, third clarinets, bass clarinets, tenor saxophones and first horn have eighths and sixteenths, while the accompaniment is in half notes—and opposing half notes at that.

Constructive Approaches to Rhythmic Precision

The greatest aid to precision is rhythmic accuracy. In this context there is no better solution than the use of a metronome, both in private practice and in group practice. There should be

Prelude and Fugue in G minor—rehearsal number 9

Flute
1st Clarinet
2nd Clarinet
3rd Clarinet

Bass Clarinet
Baritone
3rd Trombone
Bass

Alto Clarinet
Tenor Saxophone
1st Horn
2nd Horn
3rd Horn
1st Trombone
2nd Trombone

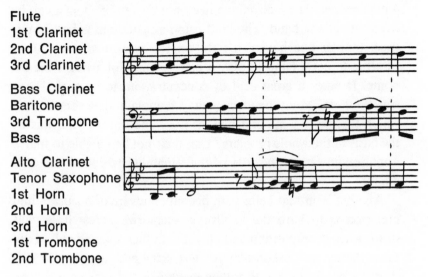

ILLUSTRATION 7-1

Prelude and Fugue in G minor—rehearsal number 10

Engl. Horn
1st Bassoon
3rd Clarinet
Bass Clarinet
1st Horn

Flute
Oboe
Eb Clarinet
1st Clarinet

2nd Clarinet
Alto Clarinet
1st Alto Sax
2nd Alto Sax

ILLUSTRATION 7-2

no reason why a band cannot play a composition while following a metronome. The metronome need not be amplified so it can be heard above the band. The kind using a pendulum is best in this case, though one having a light on top is also valuable. It is possible to get a band to play a march while following a metronome. It takes a great deal of concentration, to be sure, but it can be done. Many bandsmen may complain that they cannot watch the metronome and play at the same time. Could this be the basis of the whole problem? Can their not being able to follow a metronome be at the root of their inability to follow the conductor?

Another item that helps with becoming aware of accuracy and precision is to have the bandsmen memorize a few lines of a slow-moving composition and play it with their eyes closed. Many times the ear will become more alert if the eyes are closed. This is also a good practice to follow using isolated players, i.e., one cornet, one trombone, one horn, one clarinet, etc.

This also helps in awakening the bandsmen to the qualities of good and poor precision. While one section is practicing, the rest can be encouraged to listen by having them participate rather than just sit idle. Have those not playing grade the rest by closing their eyes (for better listening) and raising their hands into the air. They are to give points for the performances being given, like bidding on the stock market. One finger indicates an "A" or excellent performance, two fingers a "B" or good performance, etc. They should be instructed to change the number of fingers depending upon how the sound is going from moment to moment. A charted record could be kept over a period of time to see which section attains the highest degree of precision.

To help improve the accuracy of sustained tones, i.e., keeping them rhythmically synchronized with a moving melody line, the following could be done for practice purposes: Have the persons playing sustained tones articulate at the rhythmic speed of the melody. If the melody is basically in eighth notes and the accompaniment is in half notes, have the half note players break up their rhythm into four eighths per half note. If the reverse is true—if there is a sustained melody that constantly lags in tempo that is supported by a rhythmic accompaniment—make the melody into a rhythmic variation of the accompaniment, i.e., if the rhythmic accompaniment is in eighth notes have the melody break up their figures into eighth notes also.

The Basic Attack

Many bands could immediately obtain a higher rating at festivals or contests if the group could produce a good ensemble attack. Though there is no single style of attack there must be a point of reference from which the instrumentalists can work.

There are four steps necessary to making a good first attack:

First.......The embouchure must be properly set. The degree of tension and/or relaxation is different depending upon which pitch is to be played. This is as true on woodwinds as on brass. Granted, the variances on woodwinds are not as great or as crucial as on brass.

Second.....The tongue is placed on the reed or at the roof of the mouth.

Third......The diaphragm is activated, creating the *exact* amount of compression necessary to create the particular tone to be played. As with the embouchure, there *are* different amounts of compression needed for tones in different registers.

Fourth.....The tongue is lowered from its compression-creating position. One must be certain that the tongue is merely lowered or released or withdrawn and that the diaphragm does not give out with a microscopic burst of air at the instant of the release.

These four steps should be memorized by the bandsmen and some time spent practicing them in slow motion. It should be remembered that these four steps are *only* for the basic attack. It is not the same process as tonguing within a series of tones, but is a considerably different technic.

A good rehearsal technic for improving the band's ability in this area is to take a composition's first tone and play it several times, each time pointing out which section is too loud, which section is too late or too early, etc. While doing this be sure to insist that *every eye be on the baton*. At the same time the eyes of the director should be on the instrumentalists. Practicing this with the group gives the director some time to check his own technic.

How to Open

A sure method of accomplishing a good opening to any composition is to have the bandsmen memorize the first few notes so they can look directly at the baton. This also means that the director cannot bury his head in the score. For further practice, take several compositions to be played at the next concert and play just the first tones of each in succession. At first the director should describe the mood, style and dynamic level that has to be accomplished in each case.

Sometimes it becomes necessary to edit certain passages in music to gain precision and clarity. Often certain numbers or groups of instruments need to be eliminated. This is an accepted procedure. Furtwangler and Toscanini in several instances have edited works by Beethoven to the extent that these "improvements" have become a tradition.

A conductor who knows his group thoroughly should not hesitate to use his imagination and creativity to bring out the best in his band, whether it is by encouraging the players to play their best or by helping them sound their best by making over an arrangement to allow them to put their best foot forward.

Many compositions, especially those designed specifically for school use, are by necessity over-scored. Composers and arrangers find this necessary because they have no way of knowing what instruments will be available to play various parts. Neither can they foresee which instruments or groups of instruments are going to be too weak to carry off a particular melodic or counter-melodic part.

Sticking pedantically to a commercial arrangement gives the organization a traditional band sound which does not always make use of the wonderful and varied colors available in the band. Many times the colorful sounds of the oboe, bassoon, bass clarinet, and saxophones are covered by doublings. The oboe's sound is often covered by doubling with the cornet or alto saxophone. The bassoon is completely covered by the doublings of the tenor saxophone or the euphonium. These doublings not only cover what could be interesting color combinations or contrasts in colors but also add to a muddy sounding organization.

Illustration 7-3 gives an example of how the editing out of various instruments can achieve some interesting effects. This discussion is in no way meant to cast aspersions on the writings of the particular arranger for they are excellent. It is just meant to show how one can make slight alterations in an arrangement to give the composition an interesting and unique sound for a band having quality performers in various areas or to alleviate problems where there are poor quality players in other areas.

The opening "Prelude" to the *Prelude and Fugue in G Minor* by J. S. Bach as arranged by R. L. Moehlmann (Illustration 7-3) consists of a series of one-measure echoing quarter note movements. This echoing technic, typical of Baroque music, calls for a contrast in sound from one measure to another. Depending upon the ability of the players in individual sections the following editing can be done. The first statement is made by the upper woodwinds with a sustained accompaniment by the horns and

Prelude and Fugue in G Minor

[Time: 3 Min.]

JOHANN SEBASTIAN BACH
Transcribed for Band by R. L. MOEHLMANN

ILLUSTRATION 7-3

lower brass. The answer in the second measure is the item in question. If one has a very strong baritone section, the contrast between the first measure woodwind color and the answer being given solely by the baritone section would be very interesting indeed. Having this second measure doubled by a honky tenor saxophone, a tubby baritone saxophone or a weak alto clarinet might destroy an otherwise beautiful contrast. If the baritone player is weak, by all means do not allow him to play the second and fourth measures. Another arrangement could be made whereby the reedy quality of the lower saxophones and bassoons could be an answering voice, deleting the baritone and alto and bass clarinets. If on the other hand the band possesses a very strong alto and bass clarinet section, the color contrast between the upper and lower clarinets would be interesting—deleting all but these instruments. The band director might go so far as to leave out the oboes and flutes for the first few measures. If a bassoon is used for the answer it should be balanced with the oboe sound, but, as is so often true, a poor oboe playing a predominant role at the outset of the "Prelude" can spoil the total picture of the composition.

Editing Tuba Parts

Following are some ideas suggested by Gerald C. Meyer that can improve the band's sound through editing of tuba parts:

"Because the tuba tone is by nature quite heavy, it is often necessary to cut down the number of players during soft and delicate passages. This can be done by checking the dynamics of the score and indicating how many tubas should play the part.

"Parts may be registered up or down an octave. Slurred passages occurring downward from E-flat$_2$ often do not sound clear; the section improves in sound when such passages are put up an octave. It may also be desirable to register the notes down an octave on some of the parts during a sustained passage. These lower pitches are often desirable on the fundamental tone of the chord being played.

"All E-flat parts that descend into the lower register of the E-flat tuba should be raised an octave so that they can be played more easily. Invariably when the E-flat tuba is given a BBb part, it must first be edited and put into the proper range for the E-flat tuba.

"Rapid slurred passages are rarely, if ever, acceptable when played by more than one tuba. The effect is usually cumbersome and heavy and tends to lack clarity and definition. This problem may be eliminated in any one of the following ways:

"1. If the passage is soft, the part may be played as written by one tuba, or by one tuba doubled by a contrabass clarinet.

"2. The sound of the section is often clarified and the original slurred idea of the composer maintained by having the passage tongued by all of the players except the first chair performer who plays the original slurred part.

"3. Rapid slurred passages may be clarified by slurring only a few notes rather than many. For example, slurring two and tonguing two notes is usually better than slurring all four of the group. Triplet figures are often better if the first two notes only are slurred and the third is tongued rather than slurring all three.

"In editing the parts it is important to check orchestral transcriptions very closely. In these works the tuba parts are usually the string bass line that has been registered within the tuba range. As a result they often contain many technically difficult sections that are quite acceptable when bowed or plucked on the double bass, but are very awkward and difficult for one tuba and nearly impossible for an entire section. Here it is often necessary to simplify the parts and have the tubas play fewer notes for the sake of clarity and accuracy. A good solution is to play only the notes occurring on the beats, or to play every other note of a 16th note passage. Since these parts are often doubled with the low woodwinds and euphoniums, the musical idea is not lost or hindered but improved by greater clarity and precision.[3]

---

[3] Gerald C. Meyer, "The Tuba Section," *The Instrumentalist,* XV, 4 (December, 1960), 58.

eight

Developing the Components of Good Musicianship

The word "musicianship" is used most often in connection with those things that are not of a purely technical nature. A band can give a technically accurate performance and yet have played unmusically. Such things as interpretation, phrasing, style and expression fall under the category of "musicianship," as opposed to such things as tone quality, articulation, intonation, rhythm, blend and balance, which are "technical" devices. It is, of course, necessary to have a fair degree of technical proficiency in order to execute a composition with any degree of "musicianship." It is a fact that a high degree of "musicianship" can only come through a high degree of technical facility. It can be said that musicianship is that ability wherein an individual or group can and does use various gradations of instrumental technics within proper musical contexts.

It is the phrase "proper musical context" that can cause the most controversy, especially during band contest time. The word "context" or "musical context" can be interpreted as meaning, or being synonymous with, proper "style" or "phrasing" or interpretation" or "expression" or all four combined.

These four musicianship-type words (style, phrasing, inter-

173

pretation and expression) are bound together and interrelated yet can be separate and distinct objectives for study.

Developing Your Band's Interpretive Abilities

Perhaps the most elusive musicianship-type word is "interpretation." It is often said that interpretation is that attribute of musical performance that is highly personal. It is also said that interpretations can vary widely from one conductor to another, yet be good examples of the "proper interpretation." Although this is absolutely true, it is only true if those making the statements really understand and can in their minds distinguish between those four musicianship-type words.

A prose text is a rather inadequate method by which to discuss interpretation without describing a myriad of specific items about an individual work, like "At letter A the tempo of this version slows down by four metronomic beats," "This phrase ending is extended ever so slightly beyond the rhythmic point," or "This or that note within the phrase is emphasized more than this or that note."

To really understand interpretation, or rather differences in interpretation, the reader is advised to purchase several recordings of a single work conducted by different people, listen to them ten or 20 times with a score in hand, and analyze the various renditions section by section, phrase by phrase, and even measure by measure.

This writer once wrote a paper comparing one symphony as conducted by five different persons. This was one of the most enlightening listening exercises ever experienced. It was amazing how different the renditions were. In order that there be no doubt that these were not poor "interpretations," let it be known that the composition selected was *Symphony No. 4* by Robert Schumann as performed by George Szell and the Cleveland Orchestra, Rafael

Kubelik and the Berlin Philharmonic, Otto Klemperer and the Philharmonic Orchestra of London, Erich Leinsdorf and the Boston Symphony, Paul Paray and the Detroit Symphony, Paul Kletzki and the Israel Philharmonic, and Joseph Krips and the London Symphony Orchestra.

The great problem in trying to dogmatically establish the "correct interpretation" (indeed an impossible problem) lies in the fact that many musical markings are just too indefinite. For example: *Allegro* (according to Willi Apel in the *Harvard Dictionary of Music*) means: "cheerful—Originally a designation for the joyful character of a piece; today employed to indicate quick tempo, regardless of the character and expression. . . ." The difficult question is: How fast must the tempo of a piece marked *Allegro* be played? Can a piece be played relatively slow and still sound "cheerful" or "joyful"? Frederick Kranz in his booklet "Metronome Techniques" gives metronomic settings for various tempo indications. However, these are not much more helpful than is the *Harvard Dictionary* in establishing a "correct interpretation" if indeed one wishes to try to establish a hard and fast rule. Mr. Franz, for example, lists *Allegro* as being 84 to 144 per quarter note. In essence he is saying, and rightly so, that in fact a composition can, under certain circumstances, be played relatively slow (MM = 84) and still be performed in a "cheerful" or "joyful" manner.

Carl Maria von Weber drew up a detailed list of metronomic markings for the various sections of his *Euryanthe Overture*. There is a wide variety of tempi for any indication. For example: *largo* was indicated as 84 at one point and 50 at another. *Moderato assai* is indicated as 92 at one point and 104 at another. *Andante con moto* is at one point indicated as being 72, at another as 66, and at yet another as being 80.

Similar problems arise when speaking about dynamic levels. How loud a *forte* should be is an impossible question to answer except in context. A *forte* in a march by J. P. Sousa will not be the same as in a transcription of Mozart's *Eine Kleine Nachtmusik*.

There are, however, some general items that help in establishing a "correct" style of interpretation within a very wide range of musical literacy. The "rules," though not hard and fast, are wound up in historical precedent, i.e., how has this composition or that composition been performed by "great" conductors and in what "style" is the composition written? A modern-day *Allegro* composed for a modern-day concert band would carry a much more vigorous, forceful and rapid tempo than an *Allegro* written for a chamber ensemble during the time of Haydn and Mozart. Even the dot that appears over or under notes (staccato) has a different interpretation depending upon the "style" of the composition. There are many "stylistic" considerations that carry a kind of musical rule-setting that brings to bear the correctness or incorrectness of the interpretation of a composition.

Musical Style

It is extremely important that a conductor know the impact of historical periods in the interpretation of music. Frequently when using the word "style," what is being referred to is "stylistic periods," or more specifically "styles of various historical periods."

It is important that the different stylistic periods be understood and the proper technics used in keeping with the character of the period. Whereas one gradation of technic is fine for music of the Romantic period, for example, it may or may not be acceptable for music of the Baroque period. There are two publications that come to mind that cover this phase of "musicianship" for purposes of actual performance practice: *Technique and Styles in Choral Singing* by George Howerton, published by Carl Fischer, and *Teaching Musicianship in the High School Band* by Joseph Labuta, published by Parker Publishing Company.

Though it is impossible to reduce playing with good style to some simple rules, many basic points can be introduced as rules, even though they are subject to many exceptions and varying degrees of application.

The following 23 points, set down by Thomas A. Ayres, are not listed in any particular order of importance, nor do they represent any attempt to cover all possibilities. They are intended instead to form a groundwork from which artistic development can begin.

"1. An accented note not slurred must be slightly detached from the preceding note. Shorten the note before and play it somewhat softer than the accented note.

"2. When two or more accented notes are in succession, they must be separated from each other. Each one must be shortened slightly, leaving a little 'daylight' between.

"3. In syncopated rhythms, notes starting on upbeats or offbeats should be accented. Since they are to be accented, they must also be played in a detached style.

"4. The longer notes of a phrase or rhythmic pattern must be played with more emphasis than shorter notes. The difference need not be great; this will depend upon the particular phrase.

"5. In fast or lively music or in music of light character, notes not slurred that are equal divisions of the beat must be staccato. Notes of a full beat or more must be held full value. All *alla breve*, short notes would include quarter notes, eighths, and sixteenths. The exact degree of staccato will be determined by the style of the music. Dotted eighths or dotted quarters in *alla breve* are played as long notes, not staccato.

"6. Final notes of slurred groups in lively music should be clipped off a little short. This is particularly important when the last note in the slur is followed by a staccato note; if the final note were not shortened, the next note could not be played staccato. A staccato note must have space before and after it.

"7. In a cantabile style, final notes of phrases should be

rounded off. By tapering the last note or making a little diminuendo just before the release, the phrase is made to sound more finished. Avoid leaving 'square corners.'

"8. Notes followed by rest should be held full value unless otherwise marked.

"9. Notes that are altered by accidents and fall on the beat should be slightly accented. A note that is not in the key of the passage being played is nearly always an important note and should be stressed.

"10. Accent in wind instrument playing should result mostly from increased force of breath, not from more violent action of the tongue. Percussive, explosive noises produced by hard tonguing are not musical. The accent is produced by pressing in with the abdominal muscles to speed up the movement of the air column.

"11. In ensemble playing, dissonances should be stressed. Dissonances in music of traditional harmonic structure are effective because of the satisfaction to the ear in the resolution to consonant chords. By accenting the dissonance and softening the tone slightly when moving to the chord or note of resolution, the musical effect is considerably enhanced.

"12. In ensemble playing, parts that are melodic or thematic should be brought out. Parts that accompany or are merely rhythmic or harmonic should be subdued. The thematic part may last for only two or three notes, or it may be an extended passage of many measures. The player must listen to the other parts at all times in order to judge the importance of his own part.

"13. Be sure that rests get full value. The spaces and silences between notes are just as important as the notes in conveying the feeling and mood of the piece.

"14. Don't hurry to meet important notes—final notes of phrases or movements, accented notes, accidentals, etc. They must be carefully 'placed' or even slightly delayed in order to draw more attention to their importance.

"15. Breathing must fit the phrasing. Determine where the phrases begin and end, and take breaths where they will not interrupt the feeling and flow of the phrases. In cases where the phrase structure cannot be determined with certainty, it is usually fairly safe to breathe *after* the first beat of a measure and to avoid breathing at the end of a measure.

"16. In a slow melodic piece, groups of faster notes should be played with a little rubato. Usually it will sound best if you start the fast group rather deliberately and then play the latter part of it a little more quickly.

"17. Trills of a beat or longer in melodic passages should begin with one or two slow alternations of pitch before proceeding to a rapid trill. This, however, can easily be overdone; if the change from slow to fast is too long drawn out, the effect is not good. Remember too in regard to trills that the evenness of the trill is more important than its speed.

"18. A short grace note should be softer than the note that follows. Too often the quick grace note, as the note that receives the attack, is played too loudly or with an accent. It is not the important note.

"19. A long grace note (appoggiatura) should be accented somewhat, with the following note softer. The appoggiatura is a dissonant note, and must follow the rule of dissonances in being slightly stressed.

"20. A phrase in cantabile style must be built upon with increasing intensity to its climax, then allowed to subside again. The climax, or musical high point, may be the highest note, the lowest note, one that is chromatically altered, or a point in the phrase that is distinguished in some other manner. Wherever it comes within the phrase, the playing must draw attention to it, if the phrase is to convey the meaning that the composer intended.

"21. When a theme returns later in the composition, it may be preceded by a slight ritardando. The slowing down should be slight, and just before the return, not spread out over several beats unless so marked. The ritardando prepares the listener's ear for the return.

"22. An upbeat note, or anacrusis, must be softer than the note on the beat to which it leads. This is particularly important when the upbeat and the note on the main beat have the same value. If the upbeat note is too loud, it draws attention away from the note on the main beat, which is the important note.

"23. Long notes, except at the end of a phrase, or when otherwise marked, should be sustained at an even dynamic level. They should not be allowed to diminish, or become 'wedge-shaped.' " [1]

How to Develop Phrasing

Grove's Dictionary of Music and Musicians describes phrasing as: "The shaping of melodies by stress and articulation. Just as the intelligent reading of a literary composition depends chiefly upon two things—accentuation and punctuation—so does musical phrasing depend on the relative strength of the sounds and upon their connection with or separation from each other."

In order to properly phrase on a musical instrument an individual or group must know several things: first, he must know and be aware of what a phrase is, i.e., where it begins and where it ends. Second, he must be able to tell in what direction the phrase is going, i.e., where emphasis and de-emphasis are to be placed.

Components of a Phrase

There are several ways of distinguishing a point where a phrase begins and ends. Some of these include:

1. rhythmic slow-down
2. melodic contour
3. melodic characteristics

---

[1] Thomas A. Ayres, "The Groundword of Musicianship," *The Instrumentalist,* XV, 5 (January, 1961), 40.

4. repetition
5. cadential structure

The bar-lines have no effect upon phrasing! They do help in showing whether a phrase has a masculine or feminine ending, it is true, but not necessarily where they start and stop. Phrases can start and stop at any point within a measure. Of those who are constantly stopped by bar-lines it is said their playing is being governed by the "tyranny of the bar-line," an extremely false tyrant. Note ligatures, i.e., the bars connecting the tops of eighth or sixteenth notes, in no way show or have any bearing on phrasing. The notes are printed thus merely as an aid in reading, nothing more. As a matter of fact, as will be seen later, phrases or phrase ideas frequently begin and end under or within such a series of notes.

Rhythmic Slow-down

When the rhythm has been moving along at a regular, steady pace of say quarters, eighths or sixteenths and comes to a half, dotted-half or whole note, this longer note probably marks the end of the phrase. Many times after a steady pace of notes in a series of some sort, a rest appears. If the rest is of some significant length, it is a definite mark of the end of the phrase. A line of steadily rising notes accompanied by a crescendo is a sure sign that the phrase is leading to a climax of some sort. If this climax is followed by a rest, then surely this climax is the phrase ending. However, if there is not some point of change other than a change of direction, this climax is merely a mid-point in that phrase. More often than not a phrase ending is preceded by a falling line. There are many times when a falling line seems to merge directly into a rest. If this is accompanied by a decrescendo, then the end of the phrase is definitely the note just preceding the rest or perhaps the rest itself. In a case like this the rest is very important as the actual end of the phrase and must be "played."

Melodic Contour: the Key to Proper Phrasing

Understanding the various types of melodic contours can help to avoid playing phrases in a note-by-note fashion. Noticing these contours gives an overall view of the melody thus allowing directional images to be formed in the mind. These directional images in turn allow the performer to consciously lead from and to various phrase points.

Ernst Toch was among the first to describe various melodic contours in his book, *The Shaping Forces in Music*. Elie Siegmeister went further and described nine separate patterns in *Harmony and Melody, Volume I: The Diatonic Style*. Those nine patterns are as follows:

1. The wave
2. The wave with climax
3. The rising wave
4. The falling wave
5. The arch
6. The bowl
7. The rising line
8. The falling line
9. The horizontal line

Illustration 8-1 shows a notated example of each of these.

The Wave

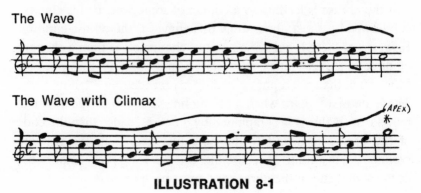

The Wave with Climax

ILLUSTRATION 8-1

The Rising Wave

The Falling Wave

The Arch

The Bowl

The Rising Line

The Falling Line

The Horizontal Line

ILLUSTRATION 8-1 (continued)

Melodic Characteristics

A change in melodic characteristics is a sure sign of one phrase ending and another beginning.

Melodies can be described as being conjunct or disjunct. The word "conjunct" refers to a type of melody that has notes in close proximity on the staff. An example of a conjunct melody is that contained in "America" (Illustration 8-2). The widest interval skip is a third.

ILLUSTRATION 8-2

A melody that jumps around is called "disjunct." An example of this type writing is the "Star Spangled Banner" (Illustration 8-3). In this there are wide leaps between notes—very few scale-wise progressions.

ILLUSTRATION 8-3

Most times a change in the melodic characteristic is also accompanied by other phrase-ending indicators. Where there is a change in character, i.e., when the melody changes from conjunct to disjunct or the reverse, this is a sure sign that somewhere between these ideas there is a phrase ending of some kind.

Repetition

Whenever two or more ideas appear in succession, whether exactly alike or slightly different, they probably can be broken into separate phrases.

Short groups of notes containing three, four or five notes must not be confused with a phrase. These short ideas are known as motives, or thematic germs, and go into making up a phrase. More will be said later on these internal parts of phrases.

Four Cadential Structures

The cadential structure of music is the best indicator of phrase progression and phrase endings.

Authentic cadence: This is a point of full stop like a period in punctuation. The formula for this is always a dominant chord moving to a tonic chord.

Half cadence: This could be likened to a comma in prose writing—a partial stop. This occurs when the phrase ends on a dominant chord.

Plagal cadence (sub-dominant to tonic): This too is a point of full stop but not necessarily a conclusive one.

Deceptive cadence: This type often serves as a joining or overlapping of phrases (dominant to sub-dominant or dominant to submediant). This is often used by a composer to sustain musical interest at a point where the authentic cadence is expected.

Internal Phrase Structures

The performer must be aware not only of the overall phrase structure but also of the various movements within the phrase. As will be seen, a phrase is a very complex movement of note to note (or rather it *should be* a movement of note to note) ending in a climax or progress from and/or to a climax point.

A phrase can consist of the following items:

1. free-flowing material
2. scalistic patterns, i.e., various scales (major, minor, whole tone, pentatonic, chromatic, etc.) as well as thirds, fourths, filled thirds, filled fourths, sequential interval skips, arpeggiated figures, etc.
3. a series of rhythmic patterns separate from or in conjunction with scalistic patterns
4. a motive
5. a motive in sequence
6. a motive with variations
7. a motive in sequence with variations
8. a motive in extended free material
9. a motive, its variation and extended free material
10. a motive and an extension (the extension can be made up of fragments of the motive in sequence and variation)

(A motive is frequently made up of materials that could be classed under items 2 and 3 of this list.)

Motivic Phrases

A "motive" is often described as a small group of notes making up a unit of musical thought. A "sequence" is the repetition of a short musical idea at different pitches, usually a second above or below. A "melodic sequence" (Illustration 8-4) is when the repetition takes place in the melodic line. Illustration 8-4 is also called a "tonal sequence." This is because the sequence progresses within the given scale or key (without any accidentals). A "tonal sequence" does not result in a modification of intervals within the sequential idea. If, on the other hand, the intervals within the sequence are kept the same (Illustration 8-5), it is called a "real" sequence. A "harmonic sequence" is when the sequential idea is passed from the melody line into another voice.

Perhaps the most famous motive is that which appears in

ILLUSTRATION 8-4 (tonal sequence)

ILLUSTRATION 8-5 (real sequence)

Symphony No. 5 by Beethoven. The entire symphony is based upon a four-note motive (Illustration 8-6).

ILLUSTRATION 8-6

How to Conduct Phrase-Note Groupings

Having a knowledge and awareness of how phrases are constructed and how the notes within a phrase relate to each other allows a performer to group notes together into minute ideas. The minute ideas can be compared to a reader who would group words within a prepositional phrase.

Illustration 8-7 shows how a single ascending scale line should have its tone linked together in the performer's mind. These small particles that make up musical phrases could be called "phrasing microbes," abbreviated in the illustrations below as "P.M."

In Illustration 8-7 the C_4 stands alone, the D leads to the E

ILLUSTRATION 8-7

which in turn leads to the F, a microscopic resting point. The G then leads by way of the A and B to the C_5. Notice that the C, D, and E do not make up a phrasing microbe even though they look as though they are connected to the note beams. Likewise, the F, G, A and B are not part of the same phrasing microbe. Comparing this to a phrase in prose, it would be like saying: "All right, now we move up to the tonic." The word "all right" is comparable to the C_4. It somewhat stands alone. Then "now we move" is comparable to the D, E, and F. The "up to the tonic" is comparable to the G, A, B, and C. Thus when playing the C_4 (equal to "all right") there would be a microscopic pause—perhaps only in the mind's thought processes. The D, E, and F (comparable to "now we move") would be a single grouped idea with the third note ("move") being the most important, the first ("now") of lesser importance, and the E ("we") of least importance. In the third phrasing microbe the last note, the C_5 (comparable to the word "tonic" in our prose phrase), would be the greatest in importance. The G relating to the word "up" would be of lesser importance, with the A and B relating to "to the " being the least important but nevertheless an important connecting link between the G (the "up") and the C_5 (the word "tonic").

Illustration 8-8 shows another musical idea broken into phrasing microbes. Notice again that the phrasing microbes cut across beams. The F stands alone; the A leads to the F by way of the G. The G would be called a "passing tone." The E then leads to the A by way of the F and G. These two notes (the F and G) could

ILLUSTRATION 8-8

also be classed as "passing tones" depending upon the chord structure underneath.

Even in a series like that shown in Illustration 8-9, the notes should be grouped together in phrasing microbes, not considered as individual tones progressing from one to another. Slurs generally do not have any effect on phrasing microbes, but merely show the type of articulation to be used. In wind instrument music slur lines are *not* phrasing lines. Slurs very often show phrasing points but not necessarily do they *always* show these points. Some series like these can have varying interpretations. Illustration 8-9 connects three sixteenths to the following, whereas Illustration 8-10 has three together—the last leading to the next three. Illustrations 8-11 and 12 show some typical sequences and how the phrasing microbes are to be treated.

Developing Musical Expression

A musical phrase, like a spoken sentence, will rise in both pitch and volume toward the apex or climax and fall off after reaching it. Each note within the phrase must be leading toward this high point or from the high point to a point of repose. In a musically shaped phrase the notes must always be aiming toward or returning from a high point.

All the notes within a phrase play a particular part in the movement of the phrase according to whether they are principal notes or "point" notes or ornamental notes, and are weighted

ILLUSTRATION 8-9

ILLUSTRATION 8-10

ILLUSTRATION 8-11

ILLUSTRATION 8-12

according to their importance or lack of importance. This weight is given most often by nuances of dynamic changes (intensity) within that phrase. On occasion rhythmical stress is also given.

Generally speaking, the longer the note the louder (more intense) it should be played, the shorter the note the softer (less intense) it should be played. This rule only applies to tones that are within and an integral part of the active melodic line. There are many exceptions to this, especially when one is playing in a large ensemble. Many times a moving line is passed from one voice to another. Sometimes the answering voice is merely a counter-like idea while the melody is sustaining. In this case the sustaining voice in the melody, though quite long, will have to be subverted to the moving line or lines.

This means then that not all the notes in a passage marked *ff* are to be played very loud. Likewise, all the notes in a passage marked *pp* are not to be played very soft. Varying the degrees of loudness and softness (intensity) is what makes for expression.

H. A. VanderCook in his book *Teaching the High School Band* sets forth some procedures that can be followed to start a band out in the direction of understanding the importance of note intensity relationships based upon rhythmic values. The book gives 14 specific methods for approach.

The Poundage System and How It Works

The various weights and balances of various notes within a phrase can be described through the use of numbers "1" through "4". Number "4" would be like giving the note four pounds of pressure—very important. The number "1" would be like giving it only one pound of pressure. These numbers do not directly relate to the traditional designations of *piano* and *forte*. Number "1" is not necessarily *pianissimo,* number "2" *piano,* number "3" *mezzo-piano,* etc. They merely represent various subtle nuances (degrees of intensity) between perhaps the levels of *piano* and *mezzo-piano* or between *mezzo-forte* and *forte.* If greater subtlety is called for, "1" might be interpreted as starting around soft *forte,* "2" as a medium *forte,* "3" as a medium loud *forte,* and "4" as a solid *forte.* In works that call for *espressivo* (and should it be a middle or late Romantic composition then even though the phrase is marked *mp*), the performer would make "1" a *pp,* "2" a *mp,* "3" a *mf,* and "4" an *f.* The exact degrees can only be decided in context and depending upon an individual's idea of the emotional content of the composition. As has been mentioned several times earlier and will be again, the "style" of the composition is a great factor in the determination of the degrees of loudness and softness used.

Illustrations 8-13 through 8-16 give a few examples of the use of the "poundage system" of numbering the notes within a phrase.

In devising an approach to teaching this the director would pass out mimeographed examples like those shown and have the bandsmen weigh each note. Individuals or the band as a whole (with the use of an opaque projector) could then be asked to play the phrases following the weights indicated. It would make

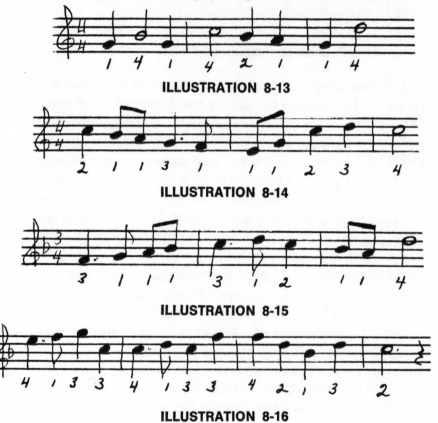

ILLUSTRATION 8-13

ILLUSTRATION 8-14

ILLUSTRATION 8-15

ILLUSTRATION 8-16

a good exercise if the director were to make up some examples of incorrect poundages and have the band try playing them. It would be extremely valuable to work out some poundage exercises using phrases from compositions being rehearsed by the band.

There is a little booklet by H. A. VanderCook that deals in detail with this "poundage system." It is entitled "Expression in Music," and it is published by Rubank, Inc.

Tempo Flexibility

In order to achieve good musicianship the performer must not only use good intonation, read around the notes, i.e., play the dynamics and emphasize the proper notes within a phrase, but must also bend the phrase and the tempo to suit the feeling and mood of the section being performed. Following is the text of an article by Ralph G. Laycock entitled "Tempo Flexibility."

"The story is told that Toscanini, in going over the score of one of Verdi's operas with the composer prior to its first performance, pointed out a place where he felt that a slight *ritard,* although not indicated, would be effective. Verdi enthusiastically agreed, commenting that it was just what he wanted, whereupon the conductor asked why it had not been written into the score. Verdi's reply was to the effect that 'if I had marked it, most conductors would have overdone the ritard.'

"Whether it be true or not, it is entirely within the realm of possibility, and, as such, points out three important considerations: (1) changes of tempo are not always marked; (2) when marked, they are often exaggerated; and (3) some composers would rather have none at all than to have them overdone. Mature composers often leave interpretative details in the hands of others who they hope will be mature performers alert to the subtleties that cannot always be put down on paper.

"Composers in earlier times were not as careful to indicate their desires as they are now. They may not have realized that they were writing for posterity—next Sunday's service was all too close at hand, and they had to get the notes copied in time for tomorrow's rehearsal. Since they were going to conduct personally and their musicians were accustomed to their manner of interpretation, minor details could safely be left for explanation during the rehearsals.

"Even careful composers often leave us very much on our own in many matters, not the least of which concern tempo and its variation.

"We cannot know for sure what the composer intended but we can develop and exercise our own best judgment with the knowledge that after all of the possibilities have been examined, it is still the conductor's obligation and privilege to do what that judgment tells him is best for his group at this time. . . .

"Leaving aside the vast area of indicated tempo changes, many of which are too often disregarded or overdone, let us consider a number of situations wherein tempo changes of varying degrees may be appropriate even though they are not indicated.

Changes of Basic Tempo

"1. Changes of texture—thinning, thickening or altering the texture through addition, subtraction or substitution of a number of instruments may indicate a new mood which may benefit from a slightly faster or slower tempo.

"2. Changes of rhythmic vitality—when a 'busy' rhythmic feeling gives way to a relaxed, less energetic one, a slightly slower tempo may be helpful in setting the new emotional climate. But be aware that the very relaxation of the rhythmic tension may in itself be sufficient and that a slower tempo could overdo the effect, producing lethargy rather than only relaxation.

"3. Style of music—music from the Renaissance and Romantic periods may, on the whole, be performed more flexibly than classic or later Baroque. Fast music usually must be more 'metronomic' than slow, but slow music with many small notes and/or repeated rhythmic patterns needs a steady pulse. Dance music which by design becomes more and more animated may call for accelerando, either section by section or a continual speeding up.

"4. Reception of a complete segment of a rhythmic piece may gain by being performed faster and more excitingly or slower and more majestically. Particularly is this true on the final portion of a sectional work such as a march.

"5. Endings—the endings of a slow piece may slow down still further in order to finish calmly; the ending of a fast piece may be accelerated in order to finish with a rousing climactic feeling; a long coda may do both in turn depending on the mood desired at any particular moment.

"6. Harmony—the amount and speed of harmonic movement may influence the tempo. For instance, a theme which has several changes of harmony per measure may have to be performed more slowly than one which has only one change per measure (or even fewer) so that the harmony can produce its full effect . . . especially when the theme is a repetition which is much more richly harmonized than an earlier version.

"7. Melody—a minor statement of a theme originally in major may possibly gain from a slower tempo if it is intended to produce a somber effect. A jagged melody with many skips may perhaps be more effective if performed a little slower than a similar one that is more step-wise.

"Whereas the above considerations refer most directly to overall changes of tempo that continue at the new pace for a number of measures or even for entire sections, there are many occasions where a more transitory dislocation of the pulse may be effective.

Momentary Changes of Tempo

"1. Slower pieces, especially those of a folk or hymn-like nature without many 'extra' notes, can usually be performed flexibly. Among the more normal places for slight rubato are climaxes, where a prolonging of the most important note(s) is effective, and at phrase endings, where a slight ritard can prove a relaxation similar to that which a period produces at the end of a sentence—a moment wherein the audience can take a mental breath and prepare for the next phrase.

"2. Fermatas—are often preceded by a slight ritard for the same reason that one slows down before bringing an automobile to a stop—there is no 'shock' when the momentum entirely ceases. But, on the contrary, there are times in dramatic pieces where the abrupt stop is precisely what is called for.

"3. Climactic notes or phrases may profit from being prolonged. In the case of high notes it may be explained as being similar to having climbed to the top of a high mountain—one would certainly wish to stand there a few moments to enjoy the view and the exhilaration before going on down the other side. Among individual notes this may take the form of an agogic accent—the prolonging of even a single important 16th note, then hurrying on—thereby giving it a desirable prominence without having to play it louder or accent it unduly.

"4. Silences—are sometimes intended to actually heighten the tension in a manner similar to a rhetorical question, or to let any tension evaporate. Proper handling of them, which may include extending them longer than may have otherwise seemed proper, may enhance their effect. But remember that the entire organization must still be 'feeling' the musical effect and act accordingly. For instance, in a tense silent pause the conductor must maintain (and insist that everyone in the group maintain) a posture of tense 'suspended animation,' otherwise the effect is utterly destroyed!

"5. Scherzando—this joking style may well call for slight rubato effects in order to maintain the light-hearted mood.

"6. Accompaniment—melodies with minimal accompaniment such as long-held notes, or with no accompaniment at all, including but not limited to cadenza-like construction, often can be performed flexibly, even if their basic tempo is quite fast.

"7. Dynamic changes—(a) *pp subito* after a loud passage may warrant waiting a moment for the sound to die away so that the first quiet notes can be heard, (b) gradual changes of dynamics may call for gradual changes of tempo, e.g., a long crescendo may be accompanied by a gradual *accelerando,* the resulting *stringendo* driving on to a climax; a long *diminuendo* may be enhanced by a gradual ritardation as an aid in relaxing the mood, (c) *crescendo-decrescendo* at the climax of a phrase may call for a broadening of the tempo in order to allow its full effect of power or heaviness.

"8. Momentary harmonic effects—a strong dissonance, an unexpected harmonic shift, etc., may often be highlighted by a slight prolongation.

"All of the above situations have had one thing in common—the tempo has been changed because the musical effect called for it, and to have failed to make such a change would have lessened the expressiveness of the composition. But there are other situations where the tempo change is necessary for purely mechanical reasons, and only if subtly handled will it avoid interference with the continuity or the expression. Indeed, it should, if possible, be so adroitly managed that it seems to actually enhance the expression. Some of these situations are:

How to Solve Common Mechanical Problems

"1. Taking a breath—many musical phrases cannot be performed in one breath, particularly those played by a solo instrument. Here, if the musical pulse will allow it, a slight ritard just before the breath is taken will make the necessary hesitation seem less obviously a delay. At times a competent performer might even be able to make such a 'natural' ritard that he would convince the audience that the ritard was called for in the original and therefore, having the time to spare anyway, he merely took a breath in the slight break that was already available to him. (Usually the previous note would have to be released somewhat abruptly, the breath taken very quickly and the next note started before the 'momentum' had entirely died.)

"2. Extreme changes of position and/or register—may take more than the 'printed' time if they are to be made accurately and confidently. If so, a slight ritard just before the shift will prepare the listener for the hesitation, serving a purpose similar to that in No. 1 above.

"3. Difficult technical passages—wherein, if the tempo need not be absolutely rigid, it is sometimes possible to 'ease' into such a spot, gain speed as the difficulty is passed, and make the passage even more exciting than it would have been had it been played 'straight.'

"Any dislocation of rhythm or tempo must be negotiated impeccably if it is to add to the musicality of the passage. But this is particularly difficult for immature groups to do unitedly, and their attempts could easily result in seemingly nothing but poor ensemble." [2]

---

[2] Ralph G. Laycock, "Tempo Flexibility—Part II," *The Instrumentalist*, XXV, 4 (November, 1970), 64.

Good Listening Is the Key to Good Playing

Music is often said to be a universal language. It is a "language" only if treated as such, i.e., presents to a listening public beautifully assimilated sounds that have style, expression and interpretation. All too often music is treated merely as a mechanical (technical) art, i.e., the right note is put at the right place within the right rhythmic framework. This may be true only because so much of the rehearsal lesson time is spent simply trying to "get 'em to learn the notes." Technical prowess of course is important; however, a simple piece of music played musically is far more enjoyable to the listener than a difficult one fumbled through. All too often the difficulty of a composition is equated with its musical quality. Though contest performance can be and is a great asset to any music program it can cause a state of confusion in regard to the kind of music to be played. Frequently, entering a more difficult classification becomes more important than doing a job more musically.

After the students learn to perform on their instruments with some technical prowess, they must be taught to bend those technics to make the language come alive. Just as there are a number of books that gradually develop a student's technical facility on an instrument, the teacher or conductor must gradually develop the student's musicianship. There are a number of publications by Belwin that can be used to begin the development of musicianship. They are: *The Magic of Tempos* by Gerald R. Prescott, *Reading Around the Notes* by Acting Ostling, *Rehearsal Fundamentals* by Fred Weber, and *Tips for Band* by Nilo Hovey.

Louis Spohr, famous violinist and composer of the 19th century, wrote the following advice for his students:

"All means of expression that help to form the finest style are successful only when refined taste presides, and when the soul of the artist is his guide. Therefore, when the student has become in some measure the master of the mechanical part of his art, he should devote himself to the cultivation of his taste, and of all that may help to increase his musical understanding. Most helpful of all to this development are frequent opportunities of listening to the performance of fine works by great artists, and careful attention to the means employed by these artists to achieve the desired effects."

When all is said and done, if a band director expects his group to play musically they must have the opportunity to hear band music played by the great bands of our day. Just as the avid football fan seeks out football games to watch, a jazz fan accumulates recordings of his favorite artists, and a stamp collector searches out and secures new and varied designs, band directors should have (and should encourage their students to have) recordings of great bands in their libraries and should travel to areas where they can hear bands perform.

Words can be used to describe many aspects of a rose: its shape, its color, its texture, the joys a dozen can bring to a sad heart; but no words will suffice for describing the delicacy of its fragrance. So too, words can be used to describe a band's seating arrangement, its beautiful uniforms, its instrumentation, the exuberance generated by its unity of action; but no words suffice for the delight of hearing a great band in performance.

Index

A

Accent, 177, 178
Accidentals, 178
Accompaniment, 148, 197
Acoustics, 137
Add-on routine, 91
Adjudicators, 105
After-beats, 150
Alla breve, 177
Allegro, 175
Alto clarinet, 33
Anacrusis, 160
Analyze, 174
Andante, 175
Announcements, 66
Appoggiatura, 179
Arch, 182
Articulation, 155
Art of Saxophone Playing, The, 114
Attack, 156, 165
Attitude, 55
Authentic cadence, 185
Authority, 157

B

Balance, 29, 76, 107, 147–171
Balanced instrumentation, 19–30
Baritone, 36, 42, 139
Bar line, 160, 181
Baroque, 195
Basketball, 27
Bass clarinet, 34, 36
Bass drum, 117, 118
Bassoon, 36, 137
Bass trombone, 37, 41
Baton, 70, 116
Batter head, 120
Beaters, 118
Beethoven, L. van, 166

Beginning-to-end, 67
Bird's-eye, 160
Blend, 77, 91–92, 106
Bore, 40
Bowl, 183
Brahms, J., 148
Brass, 19–25, 28, 31–38
  choir, 38–39
  embouchure, 116
  intonation, 137
  mouthpiece, 115, 116
  projection, 52
  seating, 47–50
  section, 38–44
  tone, 115
  valves, 137
  see also specific brass instruments
Breath control, 108, 132
Breathing, 179, 198
Bulletin board, 28

C

Cadence, 185
Cantabile, 177, 179
Cello, 35
Chord progressions, 97–98
Claesgens, G., 124
Clarinet seating, 49
  section, 20, 32–34, 133
  intonation, 109, 129, 133–134
  see also alto clarinet, bass clari-
    net, contrabass clarinet
Clarity, 166
Climax, 179, 181, 196
Competitive tuning, 92
Concert band, 21
Concert idiom, 119
Conducting, 70, 156
Conical bore, 40
Conjunct, 184

201